ABSURD ATHLETE
Ο ΑΘΛΗΤΗΣ ΤΟΥ ΤΙΠΟΤΑ

Yannis Kondos
ABSURD ATHLETE
Ο ΑΘΛΗΤΗΣ ΤΟΥ ΤΙΠΟΤΑ

᧞

Translated by David Connolly
Introduced by David Constantine

2003

Published by Arc Publications,
Nanholme Mill, Shaw Wood Road
Todmorden OL14 6DA, UK

Copyright © Yannis Kondos 2003
Translation copyright
© David Connolly 2003
Introduction copyright
© David Constantine 2003

Design by Tony Ward
Printed at Antony Rowe Ltd.
Eastbourne, East Sussex

ISBN 1 900072 76 9

The cover design is based on an idea
by Yannis Michailidis

The publishers acknowledge
financial assistance from
Arts Council England, Yorkshire

**Arc Publications 'Visible Poets' series
Editor: Jean Boase-Beier**

Series editor's note

There is a prevailing view of translated poetry, especially in England, which maintains that it should read as though it had originally been written in English. The books in the 'Visible Poets' series aim to challenge that view. They assume that the reader of poetry is by definition someone who wants to experience the strange, the unusual, the new, the foreign, someone who delights in the stretching and distortion of language which makes any poetry, translated or not, alive and distinctive. The translators of the poets in this series aim not to hide but to reveal the original, to make it visible and, in so doing, to render visible the translator's task too. The reader is invited not only to experience the unique fusion of the creative talents of poet and translator embodied in the English poems in these collections, but also to speculate on the processes of their creation and so to gain a deeper understanding and enjoyment of both original and translated poems.

Jean Boase-Beier

Περιεχόμενα

Ὁ ἐφοριακός	22
Τά παπούτσια τῆς βροχῆς	24
Ἡ μνήμη τῶν κομπιοῦτερς	28
Ἡ ξεχασμένη καμπαρντίνα	30
Χάλκινη ἐποχή	32
U2 (τρίπτυχο)	34
Τά φροῦτα καί ὁ ἄνθρωπος	38
Κενή ὥρα	40
Ἐπιτραπέζια παιχνίδια	42
Ἀπουσίες	44
Τό φίδι τοῦ σπιτιοῦ	46
Ἡ μακιγιέζ	48
Παραβάτης ἤ ''Οπως στίς βυζαντινές εἰκόνες	52
Στήν ἀναμπουμπούλα χαίρονται τά ποντίκια	54
Πρός συμμαθητάς	56
Ὑγρασία στήν πόλη	58
Τί κάνω τό σῶμα μου ὅλη μέρα	60
Ἡ ἠθοποιός Τζούλι Κρίστι μεγάλη πιά	64
Πρόχειρο διαγώνισμα	66
Παιδαγωγική	68
Τυχερά παιχνίδια	70
Θά βρέξει	72
''Υπαιθρος χώρα	74
Δωδεκαετής στήν αὐλή τοῦ Ἐπισκοπείου	76
Θά μποροῦσε νά εἶναι ταινία τοῦ Μπέργκμαν	80

Contents

Translator's preface	11
Introduction	17
The taxman	23
Shoes in the rain	25
Computer memory	29
The forgotten raincoat	31
Bronze age	33
U2 (triptych)	35
Fruit and man	39
Free time	41
Tabletop games	43
Absences	45
The house snake	47
The make-up girl	49
Apostate or As in Byzantine icons	53
Mice make the most of mayhem	55
To fellow pupils	57
Humidity in the city	59
What I do with my body all day	61
The actress Julie Christie, now old	65
Surprise test	67
Pedagogy	69
Games of chance	71
It's going to rain	73
Outdoors	75
Twelve-year-old in the bishopric yard	77
It could be a Bergman film	81

Τό μεγάλο ποτάμι τῆς μνήμης τά παρασύρει ὅλα 82
Πρόκες στά σύννεφα 84
Ὁ τυφλός καί τό σῶμα 88
Τί ἔγιναν τά παιδιά τοῦ Καρόλου Ντίκενς 90
Τό ρομποτάκι (μπαλάντα) 92
Καλοκαιράκι 94
Ὁ ἀφηρημένος ἀπό ἀγάπη ἤ Τί γυρεύει στά μέρη
μας ἡ Ἔμιλι Ντίκινσον 96
Ὁ ἀθλητής τοῦ τίποτα 100
Ψηφιδωτό στό δάπεδο βυζαντινῆς οἰκίας 104

Memory's great river sweeps all away	83
Pins in the clouds	85
The blind man and the body	89
What happened to Charles Dickens' children	91
The tiny robot (ballad)	93
Summertime	95
Distracted by love or What Emily Dickinson's doing in these parts	97
Absurd athlete	101
Mosaic on the floor of a Byzantine house	105
Biographical notes	107

Translator's preface

It is gratifying that the translators in the *Visible Poets* series should be given the opportunity to speak in their own voice and to preface their work. All translations should, in my opinion, be accompanied by a statement of the translator's aims. Not only does a statement of this kind render the translator and the translation task 'visible', it also provides the reader with the visibility required to begin to discern the 'other' text behind the translation. From the translator's point of view, all forms of translation are valid but it is also the reader's right to know what kind of translation is being offered. Once translators have stated what they set out to accomplish, and for what purpose, their work can then be read and judged in terms of the integrity of the accomplishment.

Perhaps the greater emphasis given by translators today to allowing the reader to experience the 'other' through translation stems from the fact that foreign authors are often translated today as representative of their country's literary tradition and culture, with the aim not only to present the author on the international stage but also to arouse interest in the literary tradition of which he or she is a part. This is particularly the case with literary texts written in 'languages of limited diffusion', such as modern Greek. These are certainly the two basic and underlying aims in my own translations of modern Greek poets. I do not see my role as translator as being to domesticate the other text by making it conform to the literary traditions and culture of the target language or by making it appear as if written in that language. Nor do I use it as a starting point for my own poetic aspirations. People do not read my translations because they are translations by me, in the way that they may read translations by Pound or Lowell. People read them (if at all) presumably to discover something of the quiddity and otherness of the modern Greek poets I translate.

Why we translate is one thing, how we do it is another. Over and above any particular approach or methodology (if any such exists), what is repeatedly stressed by experienced translators is the need for constant reworking and reassessment of the translated text in an attempt to make it correspond as closely as possible to the original on all levels. What are these levels? A poem contains information; it conveys the poet's ideas or sentiments and, as such, consists of some statement or message referring to the real world. It therefore functions on a semantic level. However, a poem not only informs but delights through the manner in which it informs. It may not exhibit the traditional verse forms using metre or rhyme, but, insofar as it is successful as a poem, it will be characterised by rhythm and certain formal devices which constitute its musical orchestration and allow us to talk of a poetic style. It functions, therefore, on a stylistic level. Thirdly, any poem, insofar as it functions as a poem for a particular reader, will have an emotional effect on that reader; it will have a communicative impact on the reader over and above any message or style it may possess. In other words, it also functions on a pragmatic level. If a translation of a poem is to be successful, it must, therefore, also function on these three levels, and in ways corresponding to those of the original poem.

The difficulty (impossibility?) of the task can be appreciated by considering that these three levels are not separate but interact. There are many points in a literary text where, for example, pragmatic and stylistic considerations coincide. Similarly, on a semantic level, it could be argued that the full meaning of any text lies in the intricacies of stylistic and semantic interaction (the traditional idea of the inseparability of form and content). In the transfer between languages and cultures, however, achieving correspondence on all levels will rarely be possible. So, for example, in order to maintain correspondence of sound patterns, it will be necessary to sacrifice correspondence on a syntactic or semantic level. Similarly, pragmatic correspondence is often at variance with semantic or stylistic correspondence. The demand for correspondence on all the various levels on which a poem functions creates tensions pulling in different directions. The translator has to try to balance these or, at least, to decide which will be given preference and is, therefore, involved in a continual process of negotiation.

Yet there is also one more level: what might be termed the poetic or normative level, which simply means that in addition to the difficulties involved in accounting for the poem's content, form and effect, the translator of poetry has also to produce a text that, to some extent, will meet the reader's expectation of a poem in the target culture. The poetic or normative level refers to the fact that if you want acceptance for your translations, your translated poem will have to conform (at least to some extent) to the prevalent poetic norms or poetic sensibility in a given culture. It has to have some intrinsic poetic quality defined in terms of the poetic norms of a particular time, place and tradition. This basically amounts to an acknowledgement of the expectations of the readership for poetry in a specific language or tradition. Though, of course, the translator may assume that the reader is also looking for something different or would not turn to foreign literature in translation.

Translators of modern Greek poets are perhaps further disadvantaged in their efforts to promote these poets and their tradition in the English-speaking world. The very fact of being obliged to refer to 'modern' Greek poets and not simply Greek poets is indicative of the problem. Experience has taught me that any reference to 'Greek' alone is invariably identified in the mind of the audience or readership with Greek antiquity. Many contemporary Greek poets who have failed to make any impact in English translation have undoubtedly suffered from the legacy of Greece's ancient past and from a particular perception of Greece by Westerners. The absence in their works of references to antiquity or of the kind of folkloric images of Greece created by a number of popular films conflicts with what the English-speaking reader has come to expect. Of the 'Four Evangelists' of twentieth-century Greek Poetry, C.P. Cavafy, the two Nobel laureates George Seferis and Odysseus Elytis, and Yannis Ritsos, only Cavafy is universally known. Few readers will have heard of any other twentieth-century Greek poets. A great deal of modern Greek poetry has been translated but it has failed to make any impact in the English-speaking world and contemporary Greek poets are generally conspicuous by their absence from the shelves of English bookstores and from the international stage in general.

Yannis Kondos (b. 1943) is, by general admission, one of the most notable and representative of a whole generation of Greek poets who were born at around the end of the Second World War and who first started publishing collections of their work at the beginning of the '70s. Collectively, they became known, and still are, as the Generation of the '70s or the Generation of Contention. The common socio-political dimension evident in their early work is not hard to understand given the fact that these poets reached maturity and began publishing during the political upheavals in Greece which culminated in the military dictatorship (1967-1974). However, while it is true that at the outset these poets exhibited some common characteristics in terms of theme and style, they nevertheless followed different, if parallel, paths and today the term 'generation' is no more than a genealogical characterisation. The angry cry of social protest has given way to the personal mythology of relationships, to an existential anguish and metaphysical discourse with death, and to reflections on life's absurdities, on the technological world and on the consumer society. These themes are clearly evident in Kondos' poetry, where they are presented through images linking the real and the imaginary, the mundane and the universal, the rational and the absurd.

Absurd Athlete (published in 1997) is Kondos' tenth collection of poetry, for which he was awarded the coveted State Prize for Poetry. In this collection, as in his previous ones, he takes his subject-matter from the minutiae of everyday life. For Kondos, everything, from forgotten raincoats to telephone cords, lends itself to poetry. He highlights the barely perceptible details of life which, as he puts it, will always constitute a gap in the computer's memory, but which he presents through poetry's prism and transforms through the poet's craft into metaphysical and universal statements on the condition of contemporary man in the megalopolis. For although the 'Absurd athlete' is partly the poet himself, he is above all contemporary man *running with a contrary wind... into the end's uncertainty.*

Kondos is a poet who observes and records. His belief is that the poet is not there to provide solutions, but to describe in the deepest sense. 'I don't believe,' he says 'in overly abstract poetry, but rather in narrative poetry that is based so to speak on a story with beginning, middle and end, and which has a good title. This is one of my chief concerns. And the title often constitutes a second poem within the poem.' The title in his poems in fact serves as a kind of overture to the performance which follows. For his poems have a decidedly theatrical character, sometimes even making specific references to well-known playwrights (Tennessee Williams, Samuel Beckett) in order to set the scene. Kondos is meticulous in the way he stage-directs his theme, paying attention to the scenery, lighting and music. His characters, often personas of himself, resemble empty, tragic masks delivering ironic or self-ironic monologues. The space of the drama, where the poet and his characters move and act, is the poet's own room. Yet it is this dramatic aspect which prevents the space of the poem from becoming merely a private confessional.

The theatricalness of his poetry is further enhanced by its intensely visual and iconic character. 'Some of my themes,' he says, 'are clearly painting. In many poems, the words have a chromatic quality. One phrase is red, another blue, another yellow; even an "and" can, for me, be a deep red.' And apart from these chromatic correspondences to words and phrases, it is notable how many of his poems employ actual references to colour and light. It is not without significance that his works are invariably illustrated with paintings by contemporary Greek artists.

As one might expect, given his subject matter taken from everyday life in the city, his language is simple, colloquial and unaffected. Nevertheless, as all Greek poets, he has the distinct advantage of being able to draw on all the historical phases of the Greek language (from Homer and classical Greek, through biblical and medieval Greek to the purist and popular forms of the modern era). What is an advantage for Greek poets becomes a distinct disadvantage for their translators into English, in which it is virtually impossible to reproduce this admixture of historical phases of the language, with a resulting loss in the literary effects.

Generally speaking, however, Kondos is not a poet who creates particular technical problems for his translator. His syntax is relatively simple. His poems generally exhibit a rapid sequence of short and juxtaposed images, recalling somewhat film takes and, in fact, references to the cinema and the use of its techniques constitute another constant feature of his poetry (note the overt references to Julie Christie and Bergman in the titles of two poems and the covert reference to Bergman's *Seventh Seal* at the end of the poem 'Pedagogy'). Moreover, though he is very much an Athenian poet, his poetry is not narrowly 'Greek', in the sense that it contains few of the culturally-specific references that often defy translation and require annotations. What does, however, engage the translator in the kind of constant reworking of the translated text mentioned earlier is the attempt to render Kondos' peculiar tone of voice. His many personas are invariably imbued with an underlying humour and almost childlike disposition, not, as might be expected, in order to create a sense of nostalgia for the innocence of other times, but rather as a means of moderating their inherent criticism and irony with a playful tenderness

In this, I consider myself fortunate in having been able to work closely with the poet. In fact, I wonder at the wisdom of translators who do not consult or become acquainted with the poet they are translating. For apart from being (if no longer an 'authority', then at least) a reliable source on questions of meaning and interpretation of his work, the poet is also an invaluable source of help when it comes to questions of rhythm, emphasis and tone. My regular contact with Kondos during the entire period that I worked on the translations helped to facilitate the task – not only by enabling me to check interpretations and ask for clarifications, but also by allowing me to become familiar with his humour, self-irony and childlike nature, all of which are present in his poetry, for Kondos is one of those poets who *are* as they *write*.

Kondos' first book of poetry, *Circular Route* (1970), took a well-known line of verse from the work of the Greek surrealist poet, Andreas Embiricos (1901-1975), for its motto: 'Take my word, give me your hand'. If the translator is the poet's 'other' voice, then the translation is the poet's 'other' word. I sincerely hope that this translation in the 'Visible Poets' series will result in other readers offering their hand to the poet as part of this cultural exchange. What more can either poet or translator ask?

David Connolly

Introduction

Continually, modern urban life throws up events and details that are at once real and figurative. For example, a homeless man in London, rooting through bin bags after something to eat, finds flesh he thinks suspicious. He takes it to the nearest hospital. 'Is this human?' he asks. They tell him yes. He has found a part of the dismembered body of a prostitute. That is a drastic anecdote. But cumulatively the everyday facts of life, the trash, the noise, the nervousness, the haste, the threats, if you ever pause among them and really look and listen, they shrivel the spirit almost as much as does that sad true story. Such stories, such details, true in particular, stand for a wider truth. And they affect us as both the cause and the expression of our malaise. In that combined activity – simultaneously causing and expressing – much of the virtue of good poetry resides.

Yannis Kondos, living in Athens, is very sensitive to the things that make city life an uneasy business; and very adept at converting his observations into effective imagery in poems. 'Shoes in the rain' makes a palpable anxiety out of footsteps. The speaker – victim – can always hear them, wherever he moves, however he changes. Good poetic imagery is charged with a ramifying and generalizing power. Reading this poem, you might think of any dissident glancing through the curtains to check that his surveillants are still pacing the pavement down below. Further, more absolute, the footsteps measure out a person's life: 'the sounds / begin again to the same rhythm / like hammering, like a clock.' There is a recurrent – almost a pervasive – fear of being shadowed in Kondos's poems. And by what? A hitman, a spy, a *Doppelgänger*, something that threatens, nags, troubles like conscience and the fear of death. The city, whenever there is a pause or a moment's silence, lets in such leaks and draughts of anxiety. 'It's raining again and you kiss me indifferently / gazing over my shoulder / at the next days jostling / in the doorway…'

Explicitly or not, poems are continual pointers to the better and the worse ways of being human in our day and age. That is the intrinsic ethical import of all good poems. They quicken in the reader a feeling of possible lives.

So in Kondos too, amid the welter of things assailing and corroding the spirit, there is a continual aspiration and endeavour towards a more integrated and connected life. The premise seems to be that life may be stifled entirely. Even the twelve-year-old fears this: 'The light comes down / like a press and is going to crush him. / What a small world it is ...' And the famous actress succumbs in the end to her make-up girl ('the shadow') who:

> reassures her, speaks softly to her,
> paints her nails and slowly suffocates her
> having imprisoned her in
> her very own life.

'Shoes in the rain', which initiates this collection's imagery of haunting and threat, also offers a way of answering back. The speaker so preoccupies himself with the footsteps that he converts them into a sort of energy feeding rather than devouring his own life. He says: 'So by daring the mystery / to appear, I learned a lot, saw a lot.' He opens his umbrella, strolls nonchalantly in the downpour, knowing himself surveyed, knowing his end, but greedily enjoying the present. He concludes a later poem ('What I do with my body all day') in quite a pleased tone of voice, admonishing himself:

> The twenty-four hours haven't passed
> yet, they hold lots of surprises in store
> for you, lots of chinks
> and unlimited opportunities
> for discovering sky
> and fire.

Poems lacking any such opening may demonstrate the need for it by its very absence. Brecht employs this strategy in his *Reader for Dwellers in Cities*: leaves a gap that cries out to be filled with love, solidarity, a decent humanity. The injunctions in Kondos's 'Pedagogy' express an anxiety which asks to be overridden by a bolder bid for life.

'Computer memory' lists (and incidentally celebrates) things the computer will never be able to store in its files: the caress, the kiss, the woman's stockings, the play of light on her skirt as she leaves. And for all its mathematical prowess it will never discover 'sorrow's square root'. The rest of the collection concerns itself precisely with such elusive and vital matters. Like most poets, Kondos is a searcher after vestiges and traces. Humans like to feel they make some mark by living, and may reasonably look to poetry for the record and the proof. What remains in the mirror? What is there of us in the dust? Not all hauntings are malign by any means; for very proof of existence one might wish for more of them, more ghosts, more substantial ghosts of deeds and feelings. Many poems here seem to be combing 'the circumambient universe' for private, familial and racial memories. 'Fruit and man', for example, 'Free time', 'Bronze age', 'What happened to Charles Dickens' children'. Memory and conscience are very close, of course. 'Absences' considers the dead poets and the details of human life they can no longer witness:

> the light lying in the trees
> and retaining memories;
> the espresso coffee and cigarette;
> the gloomy sky and somewhere else
> the rain.

And the poem concludes: 'But all the above / and much more / they put on the back-burner / and died.' The things they didn't say, things they put off trying to say. The onus on the living is inescapable. No excuses.

Kondos's poems make a twofold assertion: of the self against transience and death; of the self in its wish to live a connected and passionate life. In that undertaking they adopt various strategies. Altogether these are the imagination's answering back, its determined bid to effect – in Seamus Heaney's phrase – some redress. One such strategy is the adoption of personae: taxman, beast, make-up girl, for example. Thus the imagination comes at reality from novel and estranging points of view. The effort itself is valuable; it is an extension of sympathy, a part of the poem's ethical claim. Further, Kondos's poems are remarkable for their wit, their conceits, their illuminating acts of juxtaposition and montage. His grasp of modern reality is sound and obvious, but the techniques he employs to show that reality are often amusingly surreal. Thus in 'The house snake' and 'Mice make the most of mayhem'; interestingly, and perhaps more disconcertingly, the two strands – telephone cord / snake; buildings / rotten fruit – retain a good deal of separate existence, the one is not there merely to illustrate the other. This seems to increase rather than diminish (as traditional simile might) the strangeness of the world we inhabit. It must be emphasised that for all their seriousness and palpable anxiety many of these poems are droll and amusingly odd. Humour– see Beckett – is a great way of contradicting existential angst. The title poem 'Absurd athlete' works like that, the speaker even imagining himself to be 'a character out of Samuel Beckett'.

Much of what I have been saying about Kondos is summed up, better than I have been saying it, in these lines from a poem entitled 'Distracted by love':

> Stumbling
> I knock against the images' corners
> and emit sounds, astral dust
> and imagination's blood, in this land
> of noise and eventual silence.

David Connolly has done a good thing by making this compact and various collection available in English. His translations are readable with pleasure as English verse. That is always the test, and he passes it. He says in his introduction that he was anxious not to domesticate the original, the shock of the foreign being a vital contributor to success in translation. That is certainly so, in general and in this particular case. But poetry is in any case a language from elsewhere, it always does carry with it that shock, it always does depart in some peculiar way from the language we have grown too used to. We appreciate the familiar better – in its beauty and in its horror – when it is shown to us estranged. Poems can effect a renewal by saying things strangely.

David Constantine

ABSURD ATHLETE
Ο ΑΘΛΗΤΗΣ ΤΟΥ ΤΙΠΟΤΑ

Εἶδα τό ἄλλο μάτι σου
— τό μέσα, τό χωμάτινο —
νά μοῦ τραγουδᾶ
Ὅμηρο καί Τόμ Σῶγιερ.

I saw your other eye
– the inner, earthy one –
singing to me
of Homer and Tom Sawyer.

Ὁ ἐφοριακός

Ζῶ ἥσυχη ζωή.
Προσέχω τήν τροφή.
Πίνω τά χάπια μου, κοιμᾶμαι νωρίς.
Ἄχρωμος κινοῦμαι, μεταξύ δουλειᾶς
καί σπιτιοῦ. Τέτοια καί ἄλλα κοινά,
καί τρέχουν οἱ μέρες.
Ὅμως, στόν ἰσολογισμό τοῦ μήνα,
γίνομαι αὐστηρός, τσιγκούνης:
μέ τίς λέξεις, τούς φωτισμούς.
Κυνηγάω σκιές, στήνω πρόσωπα,
τά προεκτείνω στό ἔπακρο τῆς ἀντοχῆς τους,
ἀλλά καί τῆς ἀντοχῆς μου. Σέ ὅλα βάζω
μουσική. Τήν πιό ἀνόμοια.
Φέρνω θύελλες μέ ἥσυχο οὐρανό.
Κανείς δέν μοῦ χρωστάει τίποτα.
Ἀλλά ἐγώ, ὑπακούοντας σέ ἕναν
ἄγνωστο ἀρχιλογιστή, δίνω κάθε ὥρα
τούς λογαριασμούς καθαρά γραμμένους
καί πάντα ἐλλειπτικούς. Φαίνεται κάπου
χρωστάω καί μέ σταθερό χέρι
καταγράφω τίς διακυμάνσεις
τῆς ψυχῆς μου.

The taxman

I lead a quiet life,
watch my diet,
take my pills, sleep early.
Lacklustre, I move between work
and home. All this and such like,
and the days race past.
But, for the monthly accounts
I become strict, mean:
with words, the lighting.
I chase shadows, create characters,
stretch them to the edge of their endurance,
and mine too. I set them all
to music. The most incongruous kind.
I bring storms to an untroubled sky.
No one owes me anything.
Though, obedient to some
unknown chief accountant, I hourly submit
the accounts clearly written
and always in deficit. Somewhere it seems
I owe something and with a steady hand
I record the fluctuations
in my soul.

Τά παπούτσια τῆς βροχῆς

Τά ἀκούω ρυθμικά, νά μέ κυκλώνουν.
Ἀπομακρύνονται, πλησιάζουν, καρφώνοντας
τόν ἀέρα γύρω μου. Λουστρίνια, σεβρώ ἤ
ἀπό δέρμα φιδιοῦ. Ἔρχονται, ἐπανέρχονται,
βαδίζουν προπολεμικά, φέρνουν φόβο
καί τό γκρίζο στόν ὁρίζοντα. Πλάγια βροχή,
μέ φωνές παλιές, νέες, καί πάλι παλιές.
Ὁ ἐπίμονος κρότος θυμίζει ἀμερικάνικες
ταινίες, σφυρίγματα τραίνων καί πυροβολισμούς.
Σβήνουν σάν νότες τά πατήματα
καί ἔρχονται πάλι πέτρες πού κατρακυλᾶνε.
Ἀλλάζω σπίτι — ἀλλάζω ἰδέες,
πάντα μέ τριγυρίζουν.
Κοιτάζω ἀπό τό παράθυρο: σκοτάδι, ἀστραπές
καί μιά φιγούρα, ἕνα τσιγάρο, σκιά ἤ σκιές
πού κοιτάζουν πρός τό μέρος μου.
Μετά σβήνουν ὅλα καί ἀρχίζουν πάλι
στόν ἴδιο ρυθμό τά κτυπήματα,
σάν νά καρφώνουν κάτι, σάν ρολόι.
Οἱ ἐποχές ἀλλάζουν ὅπως γυρίζεις σελίδα
στήν ἐφημερίδα. Ὅμως πάντα σέ ἐπιφυλακή,
μέ τό αὐτί σέ τοίχους, πάτωμα ἤ ἀέρα,
γιά νά πειστῶ ὅτι τό μακάβριο καί ἡδονικό
τάκ-τάκ θά συνεχιστεῖ.

Shoes in the rain

I hear them rhythmically, surrounding me.
They move away, come nearer, riveting
the air around me. Of patent leather, kid leather or
snake skin. They come, come again,
walk as in pre-war times, bring fear
and the grey on the horizon. Slanting rain,
with voices old, young, and old again.
The persistent clacking recalls American
films, train whistles and gunshots.
The footsteps fade like notes
and, tumbling stones, come again.
I change homes – change ideas,
They're always around me.
I look out of the window: darkness, lightning
and a figure, cigarette, shadow or shadows
looking towards me.
Then everything fades and the sounds
begin again to the same rhythm
like hammering, like a clock.
The seasons change like turning the page
of a newspaper. Though always with caution,
with ear to the walls, floor or wind,
to convince myself that the macabre and sensual
click-clack is going to continue.

Μερικές φορές σκέπτομαι μήπως εἶναι τά δικά μου
παπούτσια τά μαῦρα, τά φθαρμένα,
ἤ ἡ σκιά μου — πού πολλές φορές
μεθάει ἀπό ἔρωτα — ὄχι, ὄχι, αὐτός
εἶναι ἐπίμονος θόρυβος δολοφόνου
μέ σκοτεινή καταγωγή καί ἄσπρα μάτια.
Προκαλώντας λοιπόν νά ἐμφανιστεῖ
τό μυστήριο, ἔμαθα πολλά, εἶδα πολλά.
Ἀνοίγω τήν ὀμπρέλα μου
καί ἀνέμελα βαδίζω στόν κατακλυσμό,
ἐνῶ ξέρω ὅτι μέ παρακολουθοῦν.

Μασάω λαίμαργα τόν καιρό
καί ὅλο σέ περιμένω.

Sometimes I think that it may be my own
black, worn-out shoes,
or my shadow – that often
is drunk with love – no, no, this
is the persistent sound of a murderer
with a shady background and white eyes.
So by daring the mystery
to appear, I learned a lot, saw a lot.
I open my umbrella
and nonchalantly walk in the deluge,
though I know they're watching me.

Greedily I chew on time
and go on waiting for you.

Ἡ μνήμη τῶν κομπιοῦτερς

Τό χαδάκι στό λαιμό σου
δέν τό πιάνει τό πεδίο ἐνεργείας
τοῦ κομπιοῦτερ. Δέν μπαίνει στό
πρόγραμμά του. Ἀρνεῖται αὐτές
τίς λεπτομέρειες. Οὔτε τίς κάλτσες σου
πιάνει, γιατί τίς ἔχεις στό χέρι
καί ἀκουμπάει στόν ὦμο μου.
Τά φιλιά σου τά μεταγράφει
ὡς θερμότητα. Δέν βλέπει τόν
ἀποχαιρετισμό, τό φῶς πού κάνει
ρίγες στή φούστα σου. Οὔτε τό μολύβι
πού γράφει τίς παραγγελίες
γιά τόν μπακάλη. Κάνει ἕνα μονότονο
θόρυβο, σάν ἀνεμιστήρας, καί βγάζει
ταινίες μέ στοιχεῖα γιά πολύ σοβαρά πράγματα.
Τήν τετραγωνική ρίζα τῆς λύπης
δέν θά τή βρεῖ ποτέ. Οὔτε
τό ἐνδιαφέρει. Θά ἀνακαλύψει
πολλά καί διάφορα, ἀλλά
τά μικρά, τά μισοσβησμένα,
θά τά ἔχει σέ κενό στίς καταγραφές
μέ τά ἀθροίσματά του.

Computer memory

The caress on your neck
can't be stored in the computer's
files. Its programme
won't accept it. It rejects all such
details. It can't even store
your stockings, because they're in your hand
and that's resting on my shoulder.
It processes your kisses
as heat. It can't see the
farewell, the light making
stripes on your skirt. Or the pencil
writing out the list
for the grocer's. It makes a monotonous
noise, like a fan, and produces
disks with data on matters of great importance.
It'll never find
sorrow's square root. Nor
does it care. It'll discover
all sorts of things, but
the little things, barely perceptible,
will be a gap in its records
and its calculations.

Ἡ ξεχασμένη καμπαρντίνα

Μέσα στό καλοκαίρι, θυμήθηκα
τήν παλιά μου καμπαρντίνα.
Ύφασμα λινό μαῦρο, ὁ ἥλιος τώρα
τήν ξεθωριάζει ἀλύπητα στό νοῦ.
Εἶχε, νομίζω, αἰσθήματα. Τά γυρίσματα
τοῦ χρόνου τήν ξεπλένουν, καί αὐτή
πιστεύει ὅτι βρέχει συνέχεια. Τά φῶτα
τῶν αὐτοκινήτων γυαλίζουν ἐπάνω της.
Ἐπιστρέφει σάν φάντασμα: σέ θέατρα,
κινηματογράφους καί ἑστιατόρια. Ψάχνει
μέσα στή νύχτα γιά ταξί.
Συνέχεια ἐπιστρέφει στό βάθος
τῆς ντουλάπας καί καπνίζει
νευρικά. Οἱ ὧρες, οἱ ἐποχές
περνοῦν δύσκολα, ἀλλά ἐλπίζει
νά ἀλλάξει ἡ μόδα, νά ξαναφορεθεῖ.
Γιά κάθε ἔκπληξη, κρατάει
τό σχῆμα της, μυρίζει ἔντονα,
καί στό γιακά ἔχει πιτυρίδα
καί μερικές ἄσπρες τρίχες.

The forgotten raincoat

In the summer I remembered
my old raincoat.
Black linen fabric, now the sun
mercilessly fades it in the mind.
It had feelings, I suppose. Rinsed
by the twists of time, it thinks
it's constantly raining. Car
headlights shine on it.
Like a ghost it returns: to theatres
cinemas and restaurants. It looks
for taxis in the night.
It continually returns to the back
of the closet and smokes
edgily. The hours, seasons
pass slowly, but it hopes
that fashion will change, that it'll be worn again.
Ready for any surprise, it keeps
its shape, smells strongly,
and on its collar has dandruff
and a few white hairs.

Χάλκινη εποχή

Οἱ ἀνασκαφές ἔδειξαν τά πρωινά σου
δυσοίωνα. Τό χῶμα κράτησε τίς πατημασιές.
Στό μέτρημα, βγήκανε πέντε ἄντρες. Ὁ ἕνας,
ὁ πιό δυνατός, φοροῦσε χρυσά πέδιλα.
Αὐτός ἔσπασε τήν πόρτα, καί σκόρπισαν
οἱ ὑπηρέτριες. Μόλις εἶχες βάλει τό πόδι
στή στέρνα, γιά τό πρῶτο μπάνιο τῆς ἡμέρας.
Οἱ φωνές σου καί οἱ ἀτμοί
φαίνονται ἀκόμη στούς τοίχους.
Χάθηκαν ὅλα τά ἄλλα:
οἱ βρισιές, οἱ προσπάθειες γιά ἐξηγήσεις,
τά παρακάλια τῆς τροφοῦ,
τό τρομαγμένο πέταγμα τοῦ περιστεριοῦ.
Βρέθηκαν τά μαχαίρια, τό αἷμα,
τά μαλλιά στά χέρια του, οἱ βόγκοι σου,
ἡ βοή καί τά θρύψαλα τοῦ σεισμοῦ
πού ἔγινε τή στιγμή τοῦ φονικοῦ.

Μετά χιλιάδες χρόνια,
οἱ κατατάξεις, τά θαμπά γυαλιά, ἡ συντήρηση,
τό μουσεῖο, οἱ περαστικοί.

Bronze age

The excavations showed your mornings
inauspicious. The earth preserved the footprints.
At the count, five men emerged. One,
the strongest, was wearing gold sandals.
He was the one to break down the door, so the maids
scattered. You'd only just put your foot
in the basin, for the day's first bath.
Your cries and the steam
are still apparent on the walls.
All the rest has vanished:
the curses, the attempts at explanation,
the nurse's pleading,
the dove's terrified flapping.
They found the knives, the blood,
the hair on his arms, your groans,
the roar and remnants of the earthquake
that happened at the murder hour.

Thousands of years later,
the classifications, the opaque glass, the conservation,
the museum, the passers-by.

U2 (τρίπτυχο)

Ἕνα

Οἱ φωνές, τά πρόσωπα,
τά ζόρικα χέρια.
Λές καί ἀνοίγεις βρύση ἡ μουσική.
Τό φῶς μεγάλης νύχτας
ἤτανε ἡ ἀγκαλιά σου καί ὁ δίσκος,
καί πῶς γλιστροῦσε τό δάσος στό ρεμβασμό μου.
Τό ἄχ τοῦ ὕπνου νά ἔρχεται
ἀπό ποτάμι μέσα στό σπίτι.
Τρίβονται τά ἔπιπλα
καί τά βιβλία βγάζουν σπίθες,
ἡ φωτιά εἶναι ἀναπόφευκτη.

Δύο

Κόκκινο λιβάδι μέ λίγο κίτρινο
στίς ἄκρες, ὅταν ὁ ἥλιος εἶναι ἁπλῶς
ἕνα τόπι πού τό κλωτσᾶς
πρός τή στρογγυλή εὐχαρίστησή σου.
Γι' αὐτό τά ἔγχορδα, τά κρουστά
καί τά τύμπανα τά ἀκούει τό μάτι

U2 (triptych)

One

The voices, faces,
rough hands.
Music like turning on a tap.
A long night's light
was your embrace and the disc,
and how the woods slid into my musings.
The ah of sleep coming
from a river into the house.
Pieces of furniture rub together
and the books emit sparks,
the fire's inevitable.

Two

Red meadow with a little yellow
at the edges, when the sun is simply
a ball that you kick
for your round enjoyment.
That's why the strings, percussion
and drums are heard by the eye

καί διαστέλλεται στό ἔπακρον.
Ὁ κυματισμός τοῦ love, σκόρος,
καί μοῦ τρώει τό πουλόβερ καί τό δέρμα.
Μετά φεύγουν ὅλα φορτωμένα
σέ αὐτοκίνητο, ἀκούγονται τά λάστιχα
νά στριγκλίζουν, μιά ἰδέα μουσικῆς ἀπό μακριά,
καί δυνατή βροχή.

Τρία

Πάλι ἔρχεται πιό δυνατός ὁ ρυθμός,
ἀνεβαίνει ἀναρριχώμενο φυτό τούς τοίχους,
καί ξεχνιέμαι στό βάθος τῆς δίνης.
Τά ρολόγια μένουν πίσω.
Τροχίζει ὁ χρόνος τά ἐξαρτήματά του,
γιά νά προσαρμοστοῦν στά νέα δεδομένα.
Ἀπό κάπου ἔρχεται ἕνας ἀέρας,
δέν μπορῶ νά ἐντοπίσω ἀπό ποῦ.
Ζωγραφίζω ἀλκοόλ στά πόδια σου χυμένο,
ζωγραφίζω φωνές καί, χορεύοντας, θέλω
νά περάσει αὐτή ἡ ἀλλήθωρη μέρα,
νά ἔρθει ἡ ἑπόμενη, καί βλέπουμε.

which dilates to the full.
The undulation of *love*, a moth,
that devours my jumper and skin.
Then they all leave packed
into cars, the tyres are heard
screeching, an inkling of music far off,
and heavy rain.

Three

The rhythm comes again even stronger,
a climbing plant, it scales the walls
and I forget myself in the whirl's depths.
The clocks fall behind.
Time hones its components,
so they'll fit the new situation.
There's a breeze coming from somewhere,
I can't work out from where.
I paint alcohol spilled on your legs,
I paint voices and, dancing, I want
this cross-eyed day to pass,
the next one to come, then we'll see.

Τά φροῦτα καί ὁ ἄνθρωπος

Νερά στά πλακάκια
καί τό καλοκαίρι καραδοκεῖ
πίσω ἀπό τίς πόρτες.
Στάζει τό σῶμα σου
σκόνες, ἡλιαχτίδες καυτές
καί ἀρχαῖες. Σκιές, φωνές —
μέσα ἀπό κήπους — πολλά πετούμενα.
Ἡ γῆ στρογγυλεύει περισσότερο,
ὁ οὐρανός καθαρός, τά σύννεφα,
δεμένα στά βουνά, ἀτενίζουν
μέ λύπη τίς πόλεις.
Στούς ἀγρούς, τό χῶμα σφίγγει.
Τά φύλλα ἀδυνατίζουν. Τό φεγγάρι
κάνει χαμηλές πτήσεις. Μιά ξέρα
ἁπλώνεται πρός στιγμήν. Κάποιος
θέλει νά τραγουδήσει. Τότε ὁ ἄνθρωπος
σηκώνει τά χέρια καί κόβει. Τό χέρι
θυμᾶται τούς προγόνους του. Τό φροῦτο,
τό χάδι, τό χνούδι, τό φιλί, ὁ ἥλιος
— ἡ ζωντανή φύση τῆς ζωγραφικῆς.

Fruit and man

Water on the tiles
and the summer lies in wait
behind the doors.
Your body drips
dust, sunbeams hot
and ancient. Shadows, voices –
from inside gardens – so many insects.
The earth grows more round,
the sky clear, the clouds,
bound to the hills, gaze
sorrowfully on the cities.
In the fields, the earth tightens.
The leaves weaken. The moon
makes low flights. A shoal
spreads momentarily. Someone
wants to sing. Then the man
raises his hand and plucks. The hand
remembers his ancestors. The fruit,
the touch, the down, the kiss, the sun
– painting's *nature vivante*.

Κενή ώρα

Κρύβομαι πίσω ἀπό τό λοφάκι
τοῦ χρόνου καί μένω στάσιμος
στίς ἐξελίξεις καί στόν πολιτισμό.
Μένω πίσω καί ἡσυχάζω
ἀπό τίς διακυμάνσεις τοῦ φωτός
καί τίς ἐπίμονες ματιές σου.
Ἔρχεται ἕνα ἄσπρο,
ἕνας ἀσβέστης, ἕνα οὐδέτερο.
Ἤτανε ἀπογευματάκι,
καί πῶς νύχτωσε ἀπότομα.
Ὅπως λέμε: «Καλό δρόμο».
Κάτι σύννεφα πῆγαν
νά βελάξουν, ἀλλά δέν ἔβρεξε.
Στό σχολεῖο, ἐκείνη τήν ὥρα,
παίζαμε. Τώρα μᾶς παίζουν ἄλλοι.

Free Time

I hide behind the hill
of time and remain stationary
amid developments and culture.
I remain behind and find respite
from the light's fluctuations
and your persistent glances.
A whiteness appears,
a paleness, a blandness.
It was early evening,
and how suddenly night fell.
As we say: 'Safe journey'.
Some clouds started
to bleat, but it didn't rain.
At school, at such times,
we played. Now others play with us.

Ἐπιτραπέζια παιχνίδια

Ὁ οὐρανός στό τραπέζι μας.
Ἕνα μῆλο φωτίζει τά πρόσωπά μας.
Τό σκουλήκι γλιστρᾶ στά σύννεφα.
Κόβουμε καί τρῶμε ἀμέριμνοι.
Τό μαχαίρι στά χέρια
κάνει κομμάτια τίς ὧρες,
τίς μέρες, τό γέλιο, τίς ἀφές.
Καπνός καί καπνός
κρύβει τό πρόσωπό σου.
Σπάει καί ἡ κλωστή τῆς σελήνης
— λεμόνια κυλοῦν στό χῶμα.

Tabletop games

The sky on our table.
An apple lights our faces.
The worm wriggles in the clouds.
Unconcerned we cut and eat.
The knife in our hands
slices up the hours,
days, laughter, touches.
Smoke and more smoke
hides your face.
Then the moon's thread snaps
– lemons tumble to the ground.

'Απουσίες

'Απογευματάκι Ἰανουαρίου,
δέν στρίβω γωνίες, ἀλλά παραπατάω
σέ εὐθεῖες. Σκέπτομαι τούς πεθαμένους
ποιητές, πού δέν βλέπουν αὐτές τίς ὧρες:
τό φῶς νά κάθεται στά δέντρα
καί νά συγκρατεῖ τίς ἀναμνήσεις·
τόν καφέ ἐσπρέσο μέ τό τσιγάρο·
τόν σκοῦρο οὐρανό καί κάπου ἀλλοῦ
νά βρέχει. Θά φοροῦσαν βαρύ παλτό,
κασκόλ, καί θά βάδιζαν γρήγορα
μή τούς πιάσει ἡ μπόρα.
Σέ μιά βιτρίνα καθυστεροῦν
καί κοιτάζουν τά ροῦχα τῆς ἐποχῆς.
Θυμοῦνται τά ραντεβού τους
καί τή ροή τοῦ ἔρωτα.
Τέλος πάντων, εἶναι ἄνθρωποι
καί γυρίζουν σπίτι.
Ὅλα ὅμως τά παραπάνω
καί ἄλλα πολλά τά γράψανε
στά παλιά τους τά παπούτσια
καί πέθαναν.

Absences

Early evening in January,
I'm not turning corners, but stumbling
in straight lines. I'm thinking of the dead
poets, who can't see these hours:
the light lying in the trees
and retaining memories;
the espresso coffee and cigarette;
the gloomy sky and somewhere else
the rain. They'd be wearing thick coats,
scarves, and be walking quickly
not to be caught in the downpour.
They linger before a shop window
and gaze at the fashionable clothes.
They remember going out on dates
and the flowing of love.
Anyhow, they're human
and go back home.
But all the above
and much more
they put on the back-burner
and died.

Τό φίδι τοῦ σπιτιοῦ

Ἕρπει παντοῦ, τινάζεται, κρύβεται
πίσω ἀπό βιβλία. Πίνει τό γάλα πού τοῦ βάζω
στήν κουζίνα. Συνήθως κουλουριάζεται πάνω
στήν τηλεόραση καί κοιμᾶται. Δέν εἶναι ἕνα
ἁπλό παχύ φίδι — τῶν παραμυθιῶν τοῦ παλιοῦ
καιροῦ —, εἶναι ἕνας κροταλίας. Στήν ἀρχή,
ὅπως ἤμουνα ἀσυνήθιστος ἀπό ἑρπετά,
φοβόμουνα. Ἤμουνα καί μικρός, καί ὅταν τό βάλανε
στήν πρίζα καί ἄρχιζε νά χτυπάει, εἶχα ἐφιάλτες.
Ἄλλαζε καί χρώματα, καί μέ τρόμαζε.
Ὕστερα ὅμως ἀγαπηθήκαμε. Ἔμαθε τίς φωνές,
τίς ἀναπνοές, τούς ἀνθρώπους. Ἔμαθε νά πηγαίνει
μέχρι τόν κῆπο. Ἔκοβε ἕνα μῆλο καί τό ἔδινε
στή γυναίκα μου. Ἐπαναλαμβάνοντας, χαμογελώντας,
τήν ἱστορία τῆς Παλαιᾶς Διαθήκης. Τά πρῶτα χρόνια
ἤτανε ἄγριο. Μάλιστα, πῆγε νά πνίξει
τόν μικρό μου ἀδελφό. Τυλίχτηκε γύρω ἀπό τό λαιμό του
καί ἔσφιγγε. Τό παιδί τό γλιτώσαμε στό «τσάκ».
Μετά, ἡμέρεψε. Μέ μένα ἔπαιζε κιόλας.
Ἀλλάξαμε σπίτια, ἀλλάξαμε διαθέσεις,
πέθαναν ἄνθρωποι, πέθαναν ἔρωτες, ἦρθαν ἄλλοι.
Αὐτό, νεανικό, στιλπνό, καί μέ ἦχο δυνατό,
παραμένει ἕνα τηλέφωνο πού ἐπωάζει τήν ἠρεμία
καί τά ἀπρόοπτα τῆς ζωῆς μας.

The house snake

It slithers everywhere, darts, hides
behind books. It drinks the milk I leave it
in the kitchen. Usually it coils on top
of the television and sleeps. It's not
just an oversize snake – from the tales
of olden times –, it's a rattler. At first,
unaccustomed as I was to reptiles,
I was afraid. I was only small and when they
plugged it in and it began to rattle, I'd have nightmares.
It also changed colour, and it scared me.
Later though we became good friends. It learned voices,
breathing, people. It learned how to go
as far as the garden. It plucked an apple and gave it
to my wife. Repeating, with a smile,
the Old Testament tale. For the first few years
it was fearsome. In fact, it nearly suffocated
my little brother. It wound itself round his neck
and squeezed. The lad escaped in the nick of time.
Later, it grew tame. It even played with me.
We changed homes, changed moods,
people died, loves died, others came.
While, youthful, shiny, and with a resonant sound,
it remains a telephone that hatches the quiet
and the unexpected in our lives.

Ἡ μακιγιέζ

στή Λούλα Ἀναγνωστάκη

Ἐπιστρέφει τριζάτη — ὅπως ἡ θάλασσα —
σπίτι της. Εἶναι περασμένα μεσάνυχτα, ἄφησε
πίσω τά φῶτα καί τίς ὁμιλίες τοῦ θεάτρου.
Ἡ τσάντα μέ τά ὑλικά τῆς δουλειᾶς — ὑλικά
τοῦ φεγγαριοῦ — τῆς βαραίνει τό χέρι.
Μαζί οἱ ἀφές, ὁ καθρέφτης καί ἕνα κάψιμο
στό δάχτυλο ἀπό τσιγάρο. Θά μποροῦσε
νά εἶναι ἀπό τά Γρεβενά, εἶναι ὅμως
ἀπό τή Μυτιλήνη.
Βαδίζει τό δρόμο τῆς ἐπιστροφῆς, κοιτάζοντας
τίς ρωγμές τῆς ἀσφάλτου. Τά μαλλιά της χρῶμα
σταριοῦ, καί τό δέρμα τό ἴδιο. Τό πρόσωπο
τῆς ἠθοποιοῦ ἔχει στήν τσέπη της, νόμισμα ἀνάγλυφο.
Τό ξέρει ἀπέξω. Τίς μικρές ρυτίδες, τίς φλέβες,
τό ἐκμαγεῖο τοῦ μετώπου, τά μικρά αὐτιά,
τά ἄβαφα χείλη, τούς ψιθύρους, τά φροῦτα στό τραπεζάκι.
Φῶς τῆς ἡμέρας βλέπει σπάνια, μόνο σέ καμιά ἐκδρομή.
Τά μυστικά της εἶναι οἱ στενοί διάδρομοι καί τό καμαρίνι.
Κατά τά ἄλλα, διάγει ἤρεμη οἰκογενειακή ζωή.
Τήν πρωταγωνίστρια τήν ἀκολουθεῖ ὅπως ἡ ζέστη.
Τελευταῖα πίνει, καί τά χέρια τρέμουν λίγο
ὅταν τήν ξεβάφει στό τέλος τῆς παράστασης.
Ἡ ἄλλη τό ξέρει καί ἀπαντᾶ μέ κοφτές κινήσεις
καί ξυραφάκια-φωνήεντα πού τινάζει μέσα ἀπό

The make-up girl

to Loula Anagnostaki

Creaking – like the sea – she returns
home. It's after midnight, she's left
behind the theatre lights and talk.
The bag with her work stuff – stuff
of the moon – weighs heavy in her hand.
Along with the touches, the mirror and a cigarette
burn on her finger. She could well
be from Grevena, but she's
from Mytilene.
She walks the path of return, looking at
the cracks in the asphalt. Her hair is the colour
of corn, and her skin's the same. The face
of the actress is in her pocket, an embossed coin.
She knows it by heart. The tiny wrinkles, the veins,
the cast of the brow, the little ears,
the colourless lips, the whispers, the fruit on the table.
She rarely sees the light of day, save for some excursion.
Her secrets are the narrow corridors and the dressing room.
As for the rest, she leads a quiet family life.
She follows the leading actress like the heat.
Lately, she's taken to drinking, and her hands tremble slightly
when removing her make-up after the performance.
The actress knows and responds with sharp movements
and razor-blade vowels that she shoots through

τά δόντια. Τῆς κάνει τόν καφέ, τῆς κάνει
μασάζ. Κάθε Δευτέρα (στήν ἀργία τοῦ ἠθοποιοῦ)
χωρίζουν. Τήν ἄλλη, ξανασμίγουν. Ρουτίνα,
θά πεῖς. Καθημερινότητα, θά ἀπαντήσει τό σκοτάδι.
Δέ φέρνει ποτέ ἀντιρρήσεις. Ὑφαίνει ὅμως μέ
τήν ὑπακοή της ἱστό ἀράχνης γύρω ἀπό τήν
ἀγέρωχη γυναίκα καί οὐσιαστικά τήν ἔχει παγιδεύσει.
Ἡ στάρ φωνάζει, τρέμει, σπάει. Ἡ μακιγιέζ
(ἡ σκιά) τήν καθησυχάζει, τῆς μιλᾶ ἁπαλά,
τῆς βάφει τά νύχια καί τήν πνίγει σιγά σιγά
ὅπως τήν ἔχει αἰχμαλωτίσει μέσα
στήν ἴδια της τή ζωή.

her teeth. She makes coffee for her, gives her
a massage. Every Monday (on the actors' day off)
they separate. The next day, they're together again. Routine,
you'll say. Daily round, the darkness will reply.
She never has any objections. Yet with her obedience
she's weaving a cobweb around the
proud woman and in effect has trapped her.
The star shouts, trembles, breaks. The make-up girl
(the shadow) reassures her, speaks softly to her,
paints her nails and slowly suffocates her
having imprisoned her in
her very own life.

Παραβάτης
ή
Όπως στίς βυζαντινές εἰκόνες

Τίς νύχτες γίνομαι κυνοκέφαλος
ἀπό τόν ἔρωτά σου. Ἔτσι ἄτσαλα
τρέχω πάνω σέ κοφτερά ποιήματα.
Μοῦ δημιουργεῖς παρελθόν, κινητή ἄμμο.
Ρόζ οὐρανό καί ρόζ σκοτάδια τοῦ Ἅδη.
Ἄδει ἡ πόλη τό:
«Θανάτω θάνατον πατήσας».
Τό πέλμα σου μέ τραβᾶ
πρός τόν οὐρανό.
Πετᾶμε.
Τώρα φορῶ τά λευκά
καί σοῦ μιλῶ κατακόκκινα.
Τώρα θυμᾶμαι μέσα στά νερά
πνιγμένος.

Apostate
or
As in Byzantine icons

At night I become dog-headed
on account of your love. So that heedlessly
I run over sharp poems.
You create for me a past, quicksand.
Rosy heavens and Hell's rosy darkness.
The city sings of how He rose:
"Through death you trampled on death".
Your foot pulls me
towards the heavens.
We're flying.
Now I'm wearing white
and I'm talking to you bright red.
Now I remember
drowned in the waters.

Στήν ἀναμπουμπούλα χαίρονται τά ποντίκια

Τό καλοκαίρι τά κτίρια τσαλακώνονται
ἀπό σκιές, ἀπό μαχαιριές, ἀπό τή ζέστη.
Εἰδικά ἐκεῖνος ὁ Ἰούλιος τά μικραίνει,
τά κάνει ἐλάχιστα. Τά πατᾶνε οἱ ἄνθρωποι
σάν σάπια φροῦτα. Κρατᾶνε ὅμως τή μνήμη
στό κουκούτσι τους. Τά κλωτσᾶνε πέρα δῶθε
οἱ περαστικοί. Τρέχουν τά τρωκτικά.
Ἐκεῖνα ὅμως, μέ ἐπιμονή καί αὐτοθυσία,
φυτρώνουν πάλι στήν ἄσφαλτο.
Μεγαλώνουν μέχρι τόν Σεπτέμβριο,
τινάζονται ὥς τόν οὐρανό
καί κατοικοῦνται πάλι
ἀνάβοντας ὅλα τά φῶτα,
σφυρίζοντας σάν ποταμόπλοια.

Mice make the most of mayhem

In summer, buildings crumple
under shadows, stabbings, the heat.
July in particular shrinks them,
reduces them to almost nothing. People tread on them
like on rotten fruit. Yet they retain memory
in their pips. Passers-by kick them
this way and that. The rodents rush around.
Yet, with persistence and self-sacrifice, they
sprout up again in the asphalt.
They keep growing till September,
shoot up to the sky
and are inhabited again
turning on all the lights,
whistling like river boats.

Πρός συμμαθητάς

στόν Κώστα Μουρσελᾶ

Ψεύτικα πού ἤτανε τά χιόνια σας,
παιδιά. Λιώσανε μέ τό πρῶτο βλέμμα.
Φάνηκε τό ἀπαίσιο καύκαλο τῆς γῆς.
Τά δέντρα ὅμως, τήν ἴδια στιγμή,
ἔχουνε φύλλα καί φροῦτα.
Ζέστη μᾶς κάνει, καί ἀνοίγουμε
τά πουκάμισα, καί γελᾶμε.
Ζέστη μᾶς κάνει, καί πᾶμε στά πηγάδια,
μέ σχοινιά ἀνεβάζουμε τά παιδικά μας
λόγια. Εἶναι δροσερά καί πόσιμα ἀκόμη.
Στό οἰκόπεδο, ἄλλοι παίζουν τώρα.
Οἱ πέτρες καί τά σημάδια μας εἶναι καλά
κρυμμένα μέσα στό χῶμα.

To fellow pupils

to Kostas Mourselas

How fake your snow was,
fellers. It melted at the first look.
The earth's horrid skull appeared.
Yet, at the same moment, the trees
have leaves and fruit.
We find it hot, open
our shirts and laugh.
We find it hot and go to the wells,
with ropes we draw up our childhood
talk. It's still cool and drinkable.
Now others are playing on the lot.
Our stones and scars are well
hidden in the ground.

Ὑγρασία στήν πόλη

Καλοκαίρι, ὅπως σέ ἔργο
τοῦ Τεννεσσῆ Οὐίλλιαμς.
Καθόμαστε στή βεράντα
μέ τά φανελάκια — οἱ
γυναῖκες ἡμίγυμνες πίνουν
λεμονάδες. Σκουπίζουμε
τόν ἱδρώτα μέ χαρτοπετσέτες.
Ἡ χαύνωση μᾶς ἔχει πάρει
μαζί της καί ἀνακατεύει στήν
ὑπόθεσή μας καί τό φεγγάρι.
Ὅλα εἶναι σάπια καί
ἀσημένια. Γάτες ἐκλιπαροῦν
γιά φαγητό. Ἐμεῖς μαθαίνουμε
τούς ρόλους μας. Ὁ σκηνοθέτης
φωνάζει: «Μήν πίνετε πολλά
ὑγρά, σέ λίγο βγαίνουμε».
Κάποιος ρίχνει σκουπίδια
στό ἐνδιάμεσο τοῦ χρόνου.
Τρέχοντας νά βγοῦμε στή σκηνή,
ἀποτυπώνουμε στόν καθρέφτη — πού
μπροστά μας κρέμεται — ἕνα ἀβέβαιο
σχῆμα, μιά γραμμή, μιά σκουριά,
ἕνα φόβο γιά τά ἐπερχόμενα.

Humidity in the city

Summer, like in a play
by Tennessee Williams.
We're sitting on the veranda
in vests – half-naked
the women are drinking
lemonade. We wipe
the sweat with paper napkins.
The languor has taken us
with it and involves
the moon too in our case.
Everything is rotten and
silver. Cats beg
for food. As for us, we learn
our roles. The stage-director
shouts: 'Don't drink too much
liquid, we're on in a moment.'
Someone throws rubbish
in time's interim.
Rushing to get on stage
we imprint in the mirror – that's
hanging before us – an uncertain
shape, a line, rust,
fear at what's to come.

Τί κάνω τό σῶμα μου ὅλη μέρα

Τό καίω, τό πετάω στόν οὐρανό.
Μετά τό βάζω σέ ἕνα γραφεῖο
καί παγώνει. Κατολισθήσεις λέξεων,
ἄδεια πηγάδια καί ἔρημος χώρα
τό περιμένουν. Φεύγω ταξίδι
μέ ἄδειο τσουβάλι, πάω γιά πέτρες —
πάω γιά ἰδέες. Βρίσκω ὄαση —
βρίσκω ποιήματα. Πλένομαι, ἐξαγνίζομαι,
θυσιάζω. Τί ἔχουν δεῖ τά μάτια μου,
δέ λέγεται. Ὅμως ὁ ὁρίζοντας εἶναι πάντα
ἕνα γαλάζιο μῆλο. Οἱ ὧρες περνοῦν
ὅπως ὀδοντωτό τραινάκι. Στή σιωπή
τοῦ μεσημεριοῦ προετοιμάζει τό μέλι
τοῦ ἀπογεύματος. Δοκιμάζω φτερά,
κανένα δέ μοῦ κάνει. Γύρω στίς ἑπτά,
ἡ νύχτα ρίχνει τό λουλακί μαντίλι της
στή λίμνη· τότε πετῶ μόνος, χωρίς μηχανικά
μέσα. Τότε τό σῶμα πίνει νερό καί εἰκόνες
γιά νά περάσει τό ὑπόλοιπο. Ἡ νύχτα ἀνάβει
τά λουλούδια καί τά φροῦτα. Αὐτό παίζει
μέ ἀναστεναγμούς καί φυσᾶ νά τά σβήσει.
Μετά βρίσκει ἕνα ἄλλο σῶμα ἤ τό θυμᾶται
καί μπαίνει μέσα καί γίνονται μουσικό κουτί.
Μετά, ἔ, μετά τελειώνουν τά παραμύθια.

What I do with my body all day

I burn it, fling it up in the sky.
Then I put it in an office
and it freezes. Landslides of words,
empty wells and a wasteland
await it. I leave on a trip
With an empty sack, going for rocks –
going for ideas. I find an oasis –
I find poems. I wash, cleanse myself,
make sacrifice. What my eyes have seen
is beyond words. Yet the horizon is always
a blue apple. The hours pass
like a rack railway train. The midday
silence prepares the afternoon
honey. I try on wings,
none of them fit. At around seven,
night casts its indigo kerchief
on the lake; then I fly on my own, without mechanical
means. Then the body drinks water and images
to get through the rest. The night turns on
the flowers and fruits. The body plays
with sighs and blows them out.
Then it finds another body or remembers one
and enters inside and they become a music box.
Then, well, then the fairytales end.

Κλείνεις τά παράθυρα, βάζεις μέσα
τή βροχή καί ψήνεσαι στήν ἀλήθεια.
Τό εἰκοσιτετράωρο δέν πέρασε
ἀκόμη, σοῦ ἐπιφυλάσσει πολλές
ἐκπλήξεις, πολλές σχισμές
καί ἀπεριόριστες δυνατότητες
ἀποκαλύψεως οὐρανοῦ
καί φωτιᾶς.

You shut the windows, bring the rain
inside and stew yourself in truth.
The twenty-four hours haven't passed
yet, they hold lots of surprises in store
for you, lots of chinks
and unlimited opportunities
for discovering sky
and fire.

Ή ήθοποιός Τζούλι Κρίστι, μεγάλη πιά

στόν Κώστα Καζάκο

Κοιτάζει τόν μπλέ διάδρομο.
Οί κουρτίνες θά άνέμιζαν
έάν άνοιγαν άπότομα
τά παράθυρα. Ἐπικρατεῖ ὅμως
ήρεμία καί θερμότητα χώρου
προσεκτικά διατηρημένη. Ἔξω, ὡς συνήθως,
τά σύννεφα τρίβονται μέ τά παλιά κτίρια
καί παράγεται βροχή ψιλή, πού εἰσχωρεῖ
στίς ρωγμές τῶν τοίχων καί τῶν ψυχῶν.
Ἐκεῖνο τό ἐγγλέζικο βράδυ, μέ περίμενε.
Ὅπως ἦτανε μόνη, τραγούδησε μιά δυό
στροφές ἀπό παλιές μπαλάντες. Στήν ντουλάπα,
τά βελούδινα φορέματά της ἀναστέναζαν,
καί ἔτριζε τό ξύλο. Πῆρε τό μπράντι.
Μύρισε, ἤπιε. Τό τζάκι ἔκαιγε.
Ἔστησε αὐτί, ἄκουγε πολλούς θορύβους
τελευταῖα, κυρίως ἐρωτικούς, καί γέλια.
Πῆρε σοβαρό ὕφος, πέρασε τή σιδερένια
γέφυρα, μέ πολλές λειχῆνες καί ὑγρές πρασινάδες,
καί ἦρθε πρός τό μέρος μου: προσπαθοῦσα
νά ξεβιδώσω τή σκέψη μου ἀπό τό σῶμα της
καί νά κοιμηθῶ ἥσυχα χωρίς τά φῶτα
τοῦ κινηματογράφου.

The actress Julie Christie, now old

to Kostas Kazakos

She gazes at the blue corridor.
The curtains would billow
if suddenly the windows
were to open. But what prevails
is calm and room temperature
carefully maintained. Outside, as usual,
the clouds rub against the old buildings
producing light rain, that enters
the cracks in walls and souls.
On that English evening, she waited for me.
Alone as she was, she sang a few
verses from old ballads. In the wardrobe,
her velvet dresses sighed,
and the wood creaked. She took the brandy.
Smelled it, drank. The hearth glowed.
She strained her ear, she'd heard many sounds
of late, mainly of love, and laughter.
Adopting a serious mien, she crossed the iron
bridge, with its numerous lichens and damp vegetation,
and came towards me: I tried
to unscrew my thought from her body
and to sleep quietly without the lights
of the cinema.

Πρόχειρο διαγώνισμα

Γνωστό τό θέμα. Τόσο διαφορετικό ὅμως
κάθε φορά. Μόλις πέρασε ἡ μέρα.
Ἔπεσε ἡ ἄλλη πάνω της, ἀκούστηκε
κρότος μεγάλος καί σηκώθη σκόνη,
ἀχός ράγισε τό σύμπαν,
δέν τά μεγαλοποιῶ.
Μοῦ θύμισε ἄλλες ἀγκαλιές, ἄλλα ποιήματα,
χρώματα ξεχασμένα.
Σέ κλάσμα δευτερολέπτου,
τό φῶς ἔγινε γραμμή στόν ὁρίζοντα.
Τότε πιάνω τά ἀλλεπάλληλα
ἐκμαγεῖα τοῦ προσώπου σου
στόν ἀέρα, ταχυδακτυλουργός εἶμαι.
Τώρα πετάω σέ κενά ἀέρος, ἀργά
ἀλλά σταθερά. Σταθερά ἔρχεται ἡ νύχτα.
Βεντάλιες ἀνοίγουν κάτι πικραμένες
γυναῖκες καί κάνουν ἀέρα μέσα στά κρύα.
Ἡ βλάστηση θεριεύει καί γελᾶ.
Γι' αὐτό μή μέ ρωτᾶς πού πάει
αὐτή ἡ σκάλα. Ἡ σκάλα πάει
στόν οὐρανό, πού χτυπᾶνε ὅλα μαζί
τά τηλέφωνα.

Surpise test

The topic's familiar. So different though
each time. As soon as the day had passed.
The next fell upon it, a loud bang
was heard and dust arose,
the din cracked the universe,
I'm not exaggerating things.
It reminded me of other embraces, other poems,
forgotten colours.
In a split second,
the light became a line on the horizon.
Then I catch the successive
casts of your face
in the air, I'm a juggler.
Now I'm flying in an air pocket, slowly
but steadily. Steadily, the night approaches.
Some embittered women open fans
and swish them in the cold.
The vegetation luxuriates and laughs.
So don't ask me where this staircase
leads. The staircase leads
to heaven, where the phones ring
all together.

Παιδαγωγική

Νά πλένεις τά χεράκια σου.
Νά τρῶς τό φαγητό σου.
Νά διαβάζεις τά μαθήματά σου.
Νά ἀγαπᾶς τά ζῶα.
Νά σκοτώνεις κάθε μέρα τούς ἀνθρώπους.
Νά κοιτᾶς μπροστά τό αὔριο καί ὄχι
τό χθές, γιατί μπορεῖ νά γίνεις μουσικός.
Νά παίρνεις προαγωγή μέ τό σπαθί σου
καί τήν ἐξυπνάδα σου.
Νά μή χάνεις χρόνο.
Νά ἀποταμιεύεις.
Νά κρύβεις τίς σκέψεις σου.
Νά εἶσαι σοβαρός (τά γέλια βλάπτουν).
Νά βαδίζεις μέ προσοχή στά σταυροδρόμια.

(Καί πέρνα καμιά φορά ἀπό τό σπίτι
γιά κανένα σκάκι — μοῦ εἶπε ὁ κύριος
μέ τή μαύρη μπέρτα.)

Pedagogy

Wash your little hands.
Eat your meals.
Study your lessons.
Love animals.
Kill people every day.
Look ahead to tomorrow and not
to yesterday, because you might end up a musician.
Win promotion on your merits
and by your wits.
Don't waste time.
Save up.
Hide your thoughts.
Be serious (laughter's damaging).
Step carefully at crossroads.

(And come by the house some time
for a game of chess – the man
in the black cloak told me.)

Τυχερά παιχνίδια

Ἔχει μιά κίνηση περιστροφῆς
τό σῶμα σου, σάν νά ξεβιδώνει
φτερά ἀγγέλων καί νά τούς κάνεις
ἀνθρώπους. Ἡ ἀλήθεια εἶναι ὅτι
πάλευα μέ τά σκοτάδια καί ἀθωώθηκα,
ὅταν εἶδα τή μουσική σου.
Θνητός ἤμουνα, μέ χιόνι στά μάτια.
Κοιτάζω τή λίμνη καί ἔχω μιά λύπη,
μιά λύπη σάν παλιό γερμανικό ποίημα.

Ἔτσι κερδίζω ἕναν πόντο θάνατο
καί ἀπεριόριστη ἀθανασία.

Games of chance

Your body has a rotating
motion, as if it's unscrewing
angels' wings, and you're making them
into people. The truth is that
I struggled with darkness and was acquitted,
when I saw your music.
I was a mortal, with snow in my eyes.
I gaze at the lake and feel sorrow,
sorrow like an old German poem.

And so I win one death point
and unlimited immortality.

Θά βρέξει

Τί Σάββατο κι αὐτό.
Λιοντάρια τρῶνε τόν Σεπτέμβριο,
καί ὁ 'Οκτώβριος μᾶς καταπίνει ὅλους.
'Αντιγράφω παλιά ποιήματα
(σάν νά σπάω πέτρες).
Ξεβάφω τίς ὦρες.
Βγάζω τά χειμωνιάτικα.
Μιλάω χωρίς ἰδιαίτερη αἰτία
στό τοπίο καί στή μουσική.
Φεύγω πάλι γιά πολύ μακριά
— ἐδῶ δίπλα θά εἶμαι.
Μόνος, κατάμονος εἶμαι στήν πόλη:
λέω ὅ,τι θέλω,
περπατάω ἀσκόπως
(τά ἐπιρρήματα ἔχουν κόκκινο βηματισμό)
— ἄκου τά βήματά μου.

Εἶμαι στή φάκα πιά,
γιά τά καλά.

It's going to rain

What a Saturday this is.
Lions devour September,
and October swallows us all.
I copy out old poems
(as if breaking rocks).
I bleach the hours,
take out the winter clothes,
speak for no particular reason
to the landscape and the music.
I leave again for far off
– I'll be here close by.
I'm alone, all alone, in the city:
I say what I like,
walk aimlessly
(adverbs have a red gait)
– listen to my steps.

I'm now well and truly caught
in the trap.

Ὕπαιθρος χώρα

Κοιτάζω τή φύση. Δέν ἠρεμῶ.
Ἀγριεύω. Βγάζω πυκνό τρίχωμα.
Γρυλίζω. Μυρίζω τόν ἀέρα.
Ἔρχεται ὁ λύκος ἀπό μέσα μου.
Ἔρχονται νύχια.
Βλέπω τό φεγγάρι μέ ἀπέχθεια.
Ἡ μουσική τῶν φύλλων
καί ἡ μουσική τῶν νερῶν
(τοῦ Χέγκελ) μέ κάνουν
νά νιώθω ξένος καί γκρίζος.
Τρώω τό ἀρνάκι μου. Τρώω
τό παραμύθι τῆς Κοκκινοσκουφίτσας.
Ὅλα κοκκινίζουν γύρω μου.
Δέν ἔμαθα τόσα χρόνια τίποτα.
Ὁ πολιτισμός δέν μέ ἄγγιξε.
Φταίει ὁ ἔρωτας; Φταίει ἡ κωλοζωή,
πού σκάλωσε κόκαλο στό λαιμό μου;
Δέν ξέρω. Καί φέτος ξαμολήθηκα
στό δάσος καί ἔσμιξα μέ τήν ἀγέλη.
Ἐσένα σκέπτομαι πάλι, μέ πόση φροντίδα
θά σκουπίζεις τά αἵματα ἀπό τό στόμα μου
ὅταν γυρίσω σπίτι ἀπό τό κυνήγι.

Outdoors

I gaze at nature. I don't grow calm.
I grow wild. I sprout thick fur.
I growl. I smell the air.
The wolf appears from within me.
Claws appear.
I view the moon with revulsion.
The leaves' music
and the water music
(Handel's) makes me
feel alien and grey.
I eat my lamb. I eat
the story of Little Red Riding-hood.
Everything becomes red around me.
So many years and I've learned nothing.
Civilization has left me untouched.
Is love to blame? Is this lousy life to blame,
its bone stuck in my throat?
I don't know. This year too I dashed
into the wood and mingled with the flock.
Again I'm thinking of you, of how carefully
you'll wipe the blood from my mouth
when I return home from hunting.

Δωδεκαετής στην αυλή του Επισκοπείου

Τρέχει πάνω κάτω, ορίζοντας τόν αέρα
σέ πρίν καί μετά. Τό φως κατεβαίνει
σάν πρέσα καί πάει νά τόν συνθλίψει.
Μικρός πού είναι ό κόσμος: μέσα μιά αυλή,
ένα άνοιγμα, ένα πέρασμα, μέ ένα
πεύκο στήν άκρη. Ξυπόλητος μπαίνει
στό εκκλησάκι. Τό πέλμα του ακουμπάει
στό κρύο — στό φρύδι του κόσμου.
Ανατριχιάζει, φοβάται, είναι ερωτευμένος.
Τόν επιτιμούν οί τοιχογραφίες, τόν τυλίγουν,
τόν σφίγγουν. Θυμάται τό μάθημα
της γεωγραφίας καί θέλει νά φύγει μακριά.
Φρούτο είναι, καί τρέχει στήν κατηφόρα
τών επιθυμιών του. Χρώμα είναι,
καί θέλει νά σκεπάσει επιφάνειες καί αγάπες.
Κοντοστέκεται, ανάβει κερί. Κοντανασαίνει
μέ μάτι κυνηγού. Τό θήραμα κοιμάται
καί τό οσφρίζεται. Ξέχασε τά παιχνίδια του.
Τά φιλιά, κρυμμένα αυγά,
επωάζονται στό βλέμμα του.
Ιδρώνει καί κρυώνει μαζί.
(Ὁ ἱδρώτας ἀργότερα θά γίνει αἷμα.)
Κοιτάζει τά χρόνια νά κατρακυλούν
καί αφαιρείται. Γαλάζια μάτια,

Twelve-year-old in the bishopric yard

He runs up and down, arranging the air
into before and after. The light comes down
like a press and is going to crush him.
What a small world it is: inside a yard,
an opening, a passage, with a
pine at one end. Barefoot he enters
the tiny church. His sole rests upon
the cold – the world's brow.
He shudders, is afraid, is in love.
The frescoes rebuke him, enfold him,
squeeze him. He recalls the geography
lesson and wants to go far away.
He's a fruit and runs down the slope
of his desires. He's colour
and wants to cover surfaces and loves.
He halts, lights a candle. He pants
with a hunter's eye. The prey is sleeping
and he smells it. He's forgotten his games.
The kisses, hidden eggs,
hatch in his gaze.
He sweats and shivers together.
(Later, the sweat will turn to blood.)
He watches the years tumbling by
and his mind wanders. Blue eyes,

λευκό φανελάκι καί χορτάρι
γιά τά ἤρεμα καί τούς ἀγγέλους
πού αἰωροῦνται μέσα του.

white T-shirt and grass
for the calm and the angels
hovering inside him.

Θά μπορούσε νά είναι ταινία
τού Μπέργκμαν

Τό πρωί, λυκόφως.
Ένα ζευγάρι παίρνει τό πρωινό του.
Κοιτάνε ἀδιάφοροι τό τσάι νά ἀχνίζει.

Τό μεσημέρι, λυκόφως.
Χειμώνας καί δουλειές.
Τό σπίτι περιμένει ἀναπνέοντας νευρικά.

Τό ἀπόγευμα, λυκόφως.
Μικρή βόλτα γύρω ἀπό τό γραφεῖο.
Τά μάτια τους βλέπουν θαμπές
εἰκόνες τοῦ χθές — τίς λένε εὐτυχισμένες.

Τό βράδυ, λίγα λόγια καί λυκόφως.
Στίς ἴδιες θέσεις, ἀντικριστά κοιτάνε,
ὑποτίθεται, τή λίμνη καί τίς πάπιες.
Κάτι λένε γιά τόν πρωθυπουργό,
τίς αὐξήσεις τῶν εἰδῶν, τίς συγκοινωνίες.
Ἀπουσία ἀντί γιά νερό τρέχει
στά σώματα τοῦ καλοριφέρ,
ἐνῶ τά σώματά τους παγώνουν.
Τυλίγονται μέ τό λυκόφως
καί κοιμοῦνται.

It could be a Bergman film

In the morning, twilight.
A couple are having their breakfast.
Indifferent, they gaze at the steaming tea.

At midday, twilight.
Winter and things to do.
The house waits, breathing tensely.

In the afternoon, twilight.
A short walk round the office.
Their eyes see blurred
images of yesterday – happy ones they say.

In the evening, a few words and twilight.
In the same places, facing each other they gaze,
supposedly, at the lake and the ducks.
They speak of the prime minister,
rising prices of goods, public transport.
Instead of water, absence runs
in the radiators,
while their bodies freeze.
They wrap themselves in the twilight
and sleep.

*Τό μεγάλο ποτάμι τῆς μνήμης
τά παρασύρει ὅλα*

Ἡ μητέρα μου στήν αἰώρα
ἀτενίζει τή θάλασσα,
πού κανονικά δέν ὑπάρχει ἔξω
ἀπό τό σπίτι μας.
Πάει καί ἔρχεται, μισοφέγγαρο,
ἐκκρεμές, κορίτσι ξεχασμένο
στό δρόμο, περασμένα μεσάνυχτα.
Ὅπως αἰωρεῖται θυμίζει τό χρόνο,
τό χῶμα καί ἐγκαρσίως
τά νερά. Ἡ ὁμιλία της
εἶναι ἀπόηχος τοῦ προσώπου,
μιά σκιά τῆς ψυχῆς.
Περνάει (ἀπότομα) νέα,
ἀγέρωχη, μέ μαῦρα μαλλιά.
Μέ φωνάζει, μέ μαλώνει, νά μή φεύγω μακριά της
καί χαθῶ στόν κόσμο: ὁ χαμένος, ὁ ἀπολεσθείς,
ὁ ἄπελπις, ὁ ἀνέστιος.

Memory's great river sweeps all away

My mother in the hammock
stares at the sea,
that normally doesn't exist
outside our house.
She moves to and fro, a half-moon,
a pendulum, a girl forgotten
on the street, after midnight.
As she swings she recalls the time,
the soil and transversely
the waters. Her talk
is an echo of the face,
a shadow of the soul.
She (suddenly) passes by, young
and proud, with black hair.
She calls to me, chides, not to go too far away
and get lost in the world: lost, unwanted,
hopeless, homeless.

Πρόκες στά σύννεφα

Ξετυλίγω τήν ἱστορία μου,
καί σέ κλείνω σπίτι, σέ κοιμίζω.
Τά φῶτα τοῦ δρόμου χαμηλά.
Μιά ἐφημερίδα πεταμένη δείχνει
τή διάθεση τῆς στιγμῆς.
Μυγδαλιές ἀνθίζουν ἀπότομα,
οἱ ἀδελφές σου δακρύζουν.
Ἐσύ ἀγέρωχη κοιτάζεις
τά καθημερινά θαύματα.
Καί τί πεταλοῦδες μέσα στό σπίτι
— τά δάχτυλα τοῦ Θεοῦ μᾶς ἀγγίζουν.
Ὑποψιάζομαι ὅτι αὐτά τά πολύχρωμα
λεπιδόπτερα, αὐτές οἱ ψυχές
εἶναι οἱ λέξεις μας.
Πάλι βρέχει καί μέ φιλᾶς ἀδιάφορα
κοιτάζοντας πίσω ἀπό τήν πλάτη μου
τίς ἐπόμενες μέρες νά συνωστίζονται
στήν πόρτα. Μαζί ἔρχεται καί ἕνα ἄλογο,
ἕνα παράλογο, λευκό καί ἀγριεμένο.
Ὁ καιρός χειροτερεύει, οἱ τηλεοράσεις παίζουν
στό φούλ. Σέ ἄλλο πλάνο, εἶμαι ποδοσφαιριστής.
Μέ χιόνι, τρέχω καί κλωτσάω
τή σκέψη μου, τή στέλνω στά δίχτυα.
Κλαῖνε, οὐρλιάζουν οἱ φίλαθλοι.

Pins in the clouds

I unwind my story,
and I keep you at home, I put you to sleep.
The street lights low.
A discarded newspaper reveals
the mood of the moment.
Almonds blossom abruptly,
your sisters weep.
Proud, you gaze
at the daily miracles.
And such butterflies inside the house
– God's fingers touching us.
I suspect that these colourful
lepidoptera, these souls
are our words.
It's raining again and you kiss me indifferently
gazing over my shoulder
at the next days jostling
in the doorway. Then a mare arrives,
a nightmare, white and alarmed.
The weather worsens, the televisions are on
full blast. In another scene, I'm a footballer.
In snow, I run and kick
my thought, sending it into the net.
The fans cry and scream.

Γιατί ἐκείνη τήν παρεξηγημένη Πέμπτη,
τήν ἄχρωμη, πού σέ περίμενα,
καί συνέβησαν αὐτά τά μαγικά,
εἶδα τό πόδι τοῦ χρόνου.

Because on that lacklustre Thursday
of misunderstandings, when I waited for you,
and this magic took place,
I saw time's leg.

Ὁ τυφλός καί τό σῶμα

Αὐτή τή μέρα τήν ξέρω καλά.
Ἤτανε Μάρτιος καί εἶχα ἀπωλέσει
τήν ὅρασή μου. Ἐκείνη τή στιγμή
τά πουλιά κελαηδοῦσαν πατριωτικά τραγούδια.
Ὁ Διονύσιος Σολωμός ἔστριβε βιαστικά τή γωνία
τυλιγμένος σέ μπέρτα μέ ἀστέρια.

(Παρακάτω, στήν ἐποχή μου.)

Ξεδιπλώνω τήν ὑπομονή μου.
Εἶναι μάλλινη καί καφετιά.
Ὁ χρόνος εἶναι ριγέ.
Ὁ γιακάς τῆς καμπαρντίνας μου ξυράφι.
Τά ποιήματα, οἱ διαφημίσεις καί ὁ καπνός
τῶν λόγων σου, θά ἔλεγα χαμένη ὑπόθεση.

(Τί ψυχή ἔχει νά παραδώσει
μιά Τρίτη καί στροβιλίζεται
σκόνη στά ἔπιπλα.)

The blind man and the body

That's a day I know all too well.
It was March and I'd lost
my sight. At that moment
the birds were singing patriotic songs.
Dionysios Solomos* hurriedly turned the corner
wrapped in a cloak of stars.

(Below, in my own times.)

I unfold my patience.
It's woollen and brownish
Time is striped.
My raincoat collar a razorblade.
The poems, the adverts and smoke
from your words, a lost cause I'd say.

(Such the ghost given up
by a Tuesday and the dust
swirls up on the furniture.)

*Dionysios Solomos (1798-1857), Greek national poet.

Τί ἔγιναν τά παιδιά τοῦ Καρόλου Ντίκενς

Χάθηκαν προσωρινά, γίνανε σκιές,
μέ παρακολουθοῦν γιά δευτερόλεπτα
μέσα ἀπό τήν ὁμίχλη,
πιάνουν τήν ἄκρη τοῦ παλτοῦ μου.
Χειμώνας εἶναι γι' αὐτά, βαρύς, μέ χιόνια.
Μέ παπούτσια χαλασμένα, μέ αἰσθήματα
κουρέλια τριγυρνᾶνε ἄσκοπα στούς δρόμους,
κάτω ἀπό φανάρια τοῦ δεκάτου ἐνάτου αἰώνα.
Τό χιόνι σφυρίζει καί τά χτυπάει ἀλύπητα.
Προσπαθεῖ νά τά σβήσει ἀπό τίς σελίδες τῶν
βιβλίων. Αὐτά ὅμως ἐπιμένουν νά τριγυρνᾶνε
στή μνήμη μας, νά μᾶς τυραννοῦν, νά μᾶς συντροφεύουν.
Χλομά καί πεινασμένα μᾶς περιμένουν
στή γωνιά, μέ τούς ὤμους τους νά διψοῦν
γιά χάδι. Σούρουπο τά εἴδαμε γιά πρώτη
φορά καί μᾶς ἔφεραν τά πιό παράτολμα σχέδια.
Ἐκεῖ πού σβήνει ἡ μουσική, κρύβονται φοβισμένα
τά παιδάκια κοιτώντας τό φεγγάρι.

What happened to Charles Dickens' children

Vanished temporarily, they've become shadows,
they watch me for a few seconds
through the fog,
clutch the edge of my coat.
For them it's winter, a harsh one with snow.
With worn-out shoes, with tattered
feelings, they aimlessly wander the streets,
beneath nineteenth-century lamps.
The snow howls and lashes them pitilessly.
He tries to erase them from the pages
of the books. But they keep wandering
in our memory, tormenting us, befriending us.
Pale and hungry they wait for us
at the corner, with their shoulders longing
for a hug. We saw them at dusk for the first
time and they brought us the most daredevil plans.
There where the music fades, frightened
children hide, gazing at the moon.

Τό ρομποτάκι (μπαλάντα)

Κάτι ἔχει πάθει ὁ μηχανισμός
τῶν ὀνείρων καί βλέπω συνέχεια
τό ἴδιο πρόσωπο. Κάτι σκάλωσε
στίς ἀναμνήσεις μου καί ἕνας ἀέρας
μέ ὁδηγεῖ, ἕνα μάτσο παλιοσίδερα,
κοντά σου. Ἔτσι ἔμαθα τίς ἐξισώσεις
τοῦ μαγνητισμοῦ καί τῆς θερμότητας.
Ἐν ὑπνώσει ἔχει κάποια ἀνθρώπινα
στοιχεῖα. Ἐλάχιστα κύτταρα κινοῦνται
καί θυμοῦνται, παράλληλα στό μέταλλο
καί στό νίκελ. Παράγουν φαντασία,
πόνο καί μούδιασμα στούς κοιλιακούς
μῦς. Παίζει τό μάτι ξάγρυπνο.
Τά φωτάκια ὅλα ἀναμμένα.
Μοιάζω ἀερόπλοιο πού ἑτοιμάζεται
νά ἀπογειωθεῖ — καί πῶς φεύγουνε
τά σύννεφα. Μένω κολλημένος στή γῆ:
λαστιχένιος μετατρέψιμος, τριψήφιος
ἀριθμός καί μόνος — SWEET HEART.

The tiny robot (ballad)

Something's gone wrong with the dream
mechanism and I keep seeing
the same face. Something's snagged
in my memories and a wind
is leading me, a handful of scrap metal,
close to you. That's how I learned the equations
for magnetism and heat.
Dormant, it has some human
attributes. A few cells work
and remember, with the metal
and nickel together. They produce imagination,
pain and numbness in the abdominal
muscles. Alert the eye darts.
The tiny lights all lit.
I look like an airship preparing
to take off – and how the clouds
move away. I remain stuck on the ground:
a rubber, convertible, three-digit
number and lonely – SWEET HEART.

Καλοκαιράκι

Ὁ σκόρος ἔρχεται πάλι.
Τρώει τό τραγούδι, τίς ἐπαναλήψεις,
τίς ἐξουσίες, τά φιλιά: ὅλα
τά κάνει σκόνη. Μοιάζει μέ τό χρόνο.
Ὁ δεύτερος εἶναι ὕπουλος, εἶναι στάσιμο νερό.
Μπαίνει στό αἷμα καί τό σκουραίνει.
Ὁ ἥλιος τρυπάει τίς ντουλάπες, τά μπαοῦλα
καί τρυπώνει ὁ σκόρος. Κάνει αὐλάκια
στό μυαλό, στίς κουβέρτες πού σέ τυλίγανε
τό χειμώνα. Ὁ χειμώνας εἶναι στήν ἀποθήκη
καί περιμένει. Ὅλα περιμένουν, νά ρουφήξει
ἡ γῆ τούς χυμούς τῶν δέντρων,
νά κοιμηθοῦν τά δέντρα,
νά ξυπνήσουμε ἐμεῖς.
Γιά τήν ὥρα, κυνηγᾶμε ζωύφια καί ἰδέες.
Τόν ἴσκιο μας δέν τόν κυνηγᾶμε,
γιατί ἔγινε πλῆθος καί μᾶς παρακολουθεῖ.

Κάθομαι στό βουνό τῆς σκόνης
καί σέ ἀγναντεύω ὅπως τή θάλασσα.

Summertime

The moth comes once again.
It eats the song, the repetitions,
the authority, the kisses: everything
it turns to dust. It's like time.
This latter is insidious, it's stagnant water.
It enters the blood and blackens it.
The sun pierces the cupboards and chests
and the moth slips in. It makes furrows
in the mind, in the blankets that cover you
in winter. Winter's in the storeroom
waiting. Everything's waiting for
the earth to suck the trees' saps,
for the trees to sleep,
for us to wake.
For the moment, we're hunting bugs and ideas.
We don't hunt our shadow,
because it's become a crowd watching us.

I sit on the mound of dust
and gaze at you as at the sea.

Ὁ ἀφηρημένος ἀπό ἀγάπη
ἤ
Τί γυρεύει στά μέρη μας ἡ Ἔμιλι Ντίκινσον

Βάλε τά φτερά — τά λεπίδια σου
στίς θῆκες καί ἔλα νά μιλήσουμε
σάν ἄνθρωποι. Μήν τεντώνεις
τό τόξο τῆς ἡλικίας σου, θά τό σπάσεις.
Μυρίζει μουσική. Μέ ἄλλο μάτι βλέπω τώρα
τόν ὑδράργυρο τῆς φωνῆς σου.
Ὅλη νύχτα ἔκοβα ξύλα, ἔκοβα λέξεις
στόν ὕπνο μου. Ἔκανα μονόλογους,
καί τό χιονόνερο τοῦ ποιήματος
μοῦ τρυποῦσε τά κόκαλα καί πάγωνα.
Ὅλη νύχτα κατέβαινα στό ὑπόγειο
πού κρύβω τή σελήνη γιά νά δῶ
τό σῶμα σου. Γιά νά δῶ τίς φωτιές
τοῦ Ἀι-Γιαννιοῦ καί τόν ἴδιο τόν
Ἅγιο Ἰωάννη μέ τό κομμένο κεφάλι
στό χέρι. Ἕνα ρυάκι ρέει, ἡ Ἔμιλι Ντίκινσον
σηκώνει τό φόρεμά της καί ἑτοιμάζεται
νά τό περάσει. Μειδιᾶ. Κοιτάζει μέ μάτια
χαμηλά τό μέλλον. Ὁ σκύλος σου δέν βλέπει
τίποτα ἀπό ὅλα αὐτά. Παίζοντας σέρνει
τόν οὐρανό στούς δρόμους. Παραπατώντας
χτυπάω στίς γωνίες τῶν εἰκόνων

Distracted by love
or
What Emily Dickinson's doing in these parts

Put your wings – your blades
into their sheathes and come, let's talk
like civilised people. Don't stretch
the bow of your age, you'll break it.
It smells of music. It's with a different eye now
that I see the mercury of your voice.
All night I was hewing wood, hewing words
in my sleep. I fashioned monologues,
and the sleet from the poem
pierced my bones and I froze.
All night I kept going down to the basement
where I hide the moon in order to see
your body. To see the fires
of St. John and St. John himself
with his severed head
in his hand. A stream flows, Emily Dickinson
hitches her dress and prepares
to ford it. She smiles. With eyes lowered
she views the future. Your dog sees
nothing of all that. Playing, it drags
the sky on the streets. Stumbling
I knock against the images' corners

καί βγάζω ἤχους, ἀστρική σκόνη
καί αἷμα φαντασίας, σέ αὐτή τή χώρα
τοῦ θορύβου καί τῆς τελικῆς σιωπῆς.

and emit sounds, astral dust
and imagination's blood, in this land
of noise and eventual silence.

Ὁ ἀθλητής τοῦ τίποτα

Τρέχει. Τρέχει μέ ἀντίθετο ἄνεμο.
Περνᾶ βουνά, λίμνες, πόλεις. Δυσκολίες
καί δυσκολίες. Φωτιές, πολέμους, γκρίνιες, οἰκογένειες.
Λίγες ὀμορφιές ὅταν σταματάει νά πιεῖ νερό.
Τίς βλέπει γιά λίγο, τίς πιάνει, ξεχνιέται.
Καί πάλι τό κυνηγητό, ἡ κομμένη ἀνάσα,
οἱ ἀποσπασματικές εἰκόνες, τραῖνα πού περνᾶν
μέ χαρούμενους ἀνθρώπους. Καί αὐτός
σάν κυνηγημένος νά προσπαθεῖ ταυτόχρονα
καί ἄλλα ἀθλήματα. Νά ἔρχεται τελευταῖος
μέ τήν ψυχή στό στόμα, νά μήν τόν βλέπει
κανείς, γιατί οἱ θεατές ἔχουν ἤδη διαλυθεῖ.
Μέ βροχές, μέ χιόνια, μέ ἥλιους, τό σῶμα
ἀντέχει, τό μυαλό πετάει. Ἄλλοτε ξεχνάει –
ἄλλοτε θυμᾶται. Σέ μιά στάση γιά νά δεῖ
τό φεγγάρι, συνέχεια σκέπτεται: τό βιολέ
ἀπόβραδο, τά χάδια καί τίς ὑποσχέσεις.
Καί τρέχει, τρέχει, ἐνῶ οἱ ἄλλοι συναθλητές του
ἔχουν τερματίσει καί σάρωσαν βραβεῖα
καί ἰαχές. Αὐτός μόνος τόν κύκλο
τοῦ χρόνου τρέχει. Χρόνος σέ εὐθεία
ἤ τεθλασμένη ἤ σπείρα. Δέν κοιτάζει
πίσω τό ποίημα, γιατί τόν ἀκολουθοῦν μύγες, ἀκρίδες
καί μολυσμένος ἀέρας τοῦ πολιτισμοῦ.

Absurd athlete

He's running. Running with a headwind.
He skirts mountains, lakes, cities. Difficulties
one after the other. Fires, wars, grumbling, families.
A little beauty when he stops to drink water.
He regards it for a while, touches it, forgets himself.
Then the chase again, the heaving breath,
the fragmented images, trains that pass
with contented people. While he,
as the hunted, tries other sports
at the same time. Coming in last
with heart in mouth, unseen
by all, for the spectators have long dispersed.
With rain, snow, sun, the body
endures, the mind soars. At times he forgets –
at others he remembers. Halting to look
at the moon, he constantly recalls: the violet
evening, the caresses and promises.
And he runs and runs, while his fellow athletes
have finished and carried off the prizes
and acclaim. Alone, he runs
time's cycle. Time in a line
straight, crooked or spiral. He doesn't look back
at the poem, as he's followed by flies, locusts
and civilisation's polluted air.

Περνώντας βλέπει δέντρα καί οὐρανό,
βλέπει πουλιά, χαμογελᾶ καί λέει
νά δραπετεύσει, νά πετάξει.
Ἀλλά δέ γίνεται, εἶναι προγραμματισμένος
γι' αὐτόν τό ρόλο. Τό ρόλο τοῦ δρομέα
μέ τό ἄγνωστο τέρμα.
Νύχτα καί μέρα ἀναβοσβήνουν.
Τά μάτια του συνήθισαν σ' αὐτό τό
λυκόφως. Ἥρωας τοῦ Σάμουελ Μπέκετ
δέν τό φαντάστηκε ποτέ ὅτι θά γίνει.
Τώρα πλησιάζει σέ ἕνα σκοτάδι
πού αὐτός τό βλέπει ἄπλετο φῶς.
Φουσκωμένα τά μάγουλα ἀπό τήν προσπάθεια,
εἶναι σάν νά φουσκώνει τά πανιά τῆς
Ἀργοναυτικῆς Ἐκστρατείας. Πάει καί πάει.
Τό πέλμα θυμᾶται τό πρίν καί τό
μετά ἀμετάκλητα. Γίνεται τροχός,
βγάζει σπίθες καί πεῖσμα τοῦ ἔρωτος.
Τό τέρμα σφίγγεται βίδα
στό ἄπειρο ἢ στήν κάθε μέρα.
Ἕνας διασκελισμός καί χάνεται
στήν ἀβεβαιότητα τοῦ τέλους.

Passing by, he sees trees and sky,
sees birds, he smiles and thinks
of escaping, of flying away.
But it's not possible, he's programmed
for that role. The role of the runner
with an unknown finish.
Days and nights flash on and off.
His eyes are accustomed to this
twilight. He never imagined he'd become
a character out of Samuel Beckett.
Now he's approaching a darkness
that he sees as profuse light.
His cheeks bulging from the effort,
as if he were blowing the sails
for the Argo's Voyage. On and on.
His sole irrevocably recalls the before
and the after. He becomes a wheel,
it emits sparks and love's tenacity.
The finish tightens, a screw
in the infinite or in every day.
One stride and he vanishes
into the end's uncertainty.

Ψηφιδωτό στό δάπεδο βυζαντινῆς οἰκίας

στόν Γιάννη Μιχαηλίδη

Τό φῶς στόν κῆπο καθαρίζει τίς φωνές καί τή σκόνη.
Στό βάθος νιώθουμε τήν παρουσία του. Φαίνονται μόνο
τά μαλλιά, ἡ αὔρα καί ὀσμή λεμονιοῦ μαζί μέ
ἄνθος, τσακίζοντας τίς ἐποχές καί τίς συνήθειες.
Εἶναι δειλινό. Οἱ ἐλιές δένουν καρπό ἀπό τά
λόγια του. Δέν εἶναι καθόλου εἰδυλλιακά.
Τά ἀπέναντι βουνά ξεφουσκώνουν σάν ἀερόστατα,
τά ποτάμια γυρίζουν πίσω καί ἡ νύχτα ἔρχεται
πίσσα καίγοντας τό πράσινο, ἤ νομίζουμε; Ὅπως
καί νά ἔχουν τά γεγονότα, ἀκοῦμε τήν ὁμιλία του.
Πίσω εἴμαστε, πολύ πίσω, κρυφοί μαθητές,
μυστικά βαπτισμένοι. Κρύβουμε τό πρόσωπο
καί φανταζόμαστε τό ἀεράκι καί τή μέντα
τῶν ματιῶν του. Εἶναι ἀδύνατο νά πλησιάσουμε.
Ἄρχισε νά βρέχει. Τό χῶμα μουγκό δαγκώνει
τίς λέξεις. Κάποιος ἄναψε ἕνα κερί.
Φύγαμε ἀπό τό πορτάκι τοῦ κήπου.
Μᾶς κατάπιε τό σκοτάδι, μᾶς μαχαίρωσε ἡ φωνή.

Ἰούνιος 1992-Ἰούνιος 1997

Mosaic on the floor of a Byzantine house

to Yannis Michailidis

The light in the garden clears the voices and dust.
We sense his presence at the back. All that can be seen is
the hair, the aura and the lemon's scent as well as
blossom, crushing the seasons and habits.
It's dusk. It's by no means idyllic.
The facing hills deflate like balloons,
the rivers turn back and night approaches
pitch burning the verdure, or is that what we think? Whatever
the case may be, we can hear his talk.
We're behind, so very behind, concealed pupils,
secretly baptised. We cover our faces
and imagine the breeze and mint
of his eyes. We're unable to get near.
It began raining. Mute the earth bites
the words. Someone lit a candle.
We left through the garden gate.
We were swallowed by the darkness, stabbed by the voice.

June 1992-June 1997

Biographical notes

YANNIS KONDOS was born in 1943 in Egion in the Peloponnese though he spent much of his childhood living in various Greek towns. He settled in Athens at the age of seventeen and considers himself an Athenian. He opened and ran a successful bookshop before moving to Kedros publishers, where he has worked for twenty-five years as a reader. During this time, he also had his own radio programme on one of the national networks, has been a regular contributor with articles on literature, art and theatre to newspapers and magazines and, in recent years, has taught literature in the Kostas Kazakos Drama School. He published his first collection of poetry, *Circular Route*, in 1970 and has subsequently published a further ten collections: *The Chronometer* (1972); *The Unforeseen* (1975); *Photocopies* (1977); *In the Dialect of the Desert* (1980); *The Bones* (1982); *By an Anonymous Monk* (1985); *Gratuitous Darkness* (1989); *At the Turn of Day* (1992); *Absurd Athlete* (1997) and *The Moon's Hypotenuse* (2002). In addition, he has also published two selections of his poetry, *When a Drum is Heard over the City* (1992) and *Pins in the Clouds* (1999), a volume of essays, *The Noble Metals* (1994) and a book for children, *Aristeides, the Little Hippopotamus* (2001). His work has been translated into numerous European languages. In 1998, he was awarded the State Prize for Poetry for his collection, *Absurd Athlete*.

DAVID CONNOLLY was born in 1954 in Sheffield, England. He studied Ancient Greek at the University of Lancaster and Medieval and Modern Greek Literature at Trinity College, Oxford. He holds a doctoral degree in the theory and practice of Literary Translation from the University of East Anglia. A naturalized Greek, he has lived in Greece since 1979 and has taught translation at undergraduate and post-graduate level for many years at a number of university institutions in Greece. He has written extensively on the theory and practice of literary translation and on Greek Literature in general and has published some twenty books of translations from the work of major Greek poets and novelists. His translations have received awards in Greece, the UK and the USA.

DAVID CONSTANTINE has published half a dozen volumes of poetry, the most recent being *Something for the Ghosts,* all with Bloodaxe Books. He is a translator of Hölderlin, Goethe, Kleist and Brecht, and his translation of Hans Magnus Enzensherger's *Lighter than Air* (Bloodaxe) won the 2003 Corneliu M Popescu Prize for European Poetry Translation. He and his wife are editors of *Modern Poetry in Translation.*

Also available in the
Arc Publications
'VISIBLE POETS' SERIES
(Series Editor: Jean Boase-Beier)

No. 1
MIKLÓS RADNÓTI
(Hungary)
Camp Notebook
TRANSLATED BY FRANCIS JONES
INTRODUCTION BY GEORGE SZIRTES

No. 2
BARTOLO CATTAFI
(Italy)
Anthracite
TRANSLATED BY BRIAN COLE
INTRODUCTION BY PETER DALE
(Poetry Book Society Recommended Translation)

No. 3
MICHAEL STRUNGE
(Denmark)
A Virgin from a Chilly Decade
TRANSLATED BY BENTE ELSWORTH
INTRODUCTION BY JOHN FLETCHER

No. 4
TADEUSZ RÓŻEWICZ
(Poland)
recycling
TRANSLATED BY BARBARA BOGOCZEK (PLEBANEK) & TONY HOWARD
INTRODUCTION BY ADAM CZERNIAWSKI

No. 5
CLAUDE DE BURINE
(France)
Words Have Frozen Over
TRANSLATED BY MARTIN SORRELL
INTRODUCTION BY SUSAN WICKS

No. 6
CEVAT ÇAPAN
(Turkey)
Where Are You, Susie Petschek?
TRANSLATED BY CEVAT ÇAPAN & MICHAEL HULSE
INTRODUCTION BY A. S. BYATT

No.7
JEAN CASSOU
(France)
33 Sonnets of the Resistance and other poems
WITH AN ORIGINAL INTRODUCTION BY LOUIS ARAGON
TRANSLATED BY TIMOTHY ADÈS
INTRODUCTION BY ALISTAIR ELLIOT

No. 8
ARJEN DUINKER
(Holland)
The Sublime Song of a Maybe
TRANSLATED BY WILLEM GROENEWEGEN
INTRODUCTION BY JEFFREY WAINWRIGHT

No. 9
MILA HAUGOVÁ
(Slovakia)
Scent of the Unseen
TRANSLATED BY JAMES & VIERA SUTHERLAND-SMITH
INTRODUCTION BY FIONA SAMPSON

No. 10
ERNST MEISTER
(Germany)
Between Nothing and Nothing
TRANSLATED BY JEAN BOASE-BEIER
INTRODUCTION BY JOHN HARTLEY WILLIAMS